The SCOTT FAMILY of Shrewsbury, New Jersey

BEING THE DESCENDANTS

OF

WILLIAM SCOTT AND ABIGAIL TILTON WARNER

WITH

SKETCHES OF RELATED FAMILIES

Compiled by

Rev. Arthur S. Cole

HERITAGE BOOKS
2013

HERITAGE BOOKS
AN IMPRINT OF HERITAGE BOOKS, INC.

Books, CDs, and more—Worldwide

For our listing of thousands of titles see our website
at
www.HeritageBooks.com

A Facsimile Reprint
Published 2013 by
HERITAGE BOOKS, INC.
Publishing Division
100 Railroad Ave. #104
Westminster, Maryland 21157

Originally published:
The Register Press
Red Bank, New Jersey
1903

International Standard Book Numbers
Paperbound: 978-0-7884-5456-1
Clothbound: 978-0-7884-6976-3

PREFACE.

Charles Wagner has said that "the best possessions of a family are its common memories." To recall and preserve these common memories, many of them long since passed out of family recollection, is the purpose of the following pages. Some old family records having come into my possession, they suggested the idea of further research and ultimate preservation by the use of the printing press. More than three years have been spent in the work, and the result is presented in this compact and simple form. Records of families related by intermarriage have to some extent been included so far as they represent lines of ancestry down to the time of intermarriage. The names of nearly one thousand descendants of the William Scott who first settled in Shrewsbury are to be found in this book, and yet the list is far from complete. A longer time and wider research might have increased the number, but it has been thought best not to delay publication. To honor and preserve the memory of those who have passed beyond the veil, to foster a proper family feeling and spirit, and to keep for future generations the record of their ancestry, these pages are sent out to the many branches of the family and entrusted to their keeping.

Through the courtesy of Mr. John H. Cook, the proprietor of *The Red Bank Register*, this family history has appeared in successive issues of that publication during the current year. This has given to others the opportunity of making a number of corrections and additions. Doubtless there are still many errors, which are always seemingly inseparable from a work of this kind, and those who consult this book are asked to notify the compiler of any mistakes and to send him any additional information which they may have. All corrections and additions will be carefully preserved and used later in any revision of, or supplement to, this work which may be published. In addition to the matter published in *The Red Bank Register* and corrections thereto, this book contains a number of illustrations, a family chart, an appendix, and a complete index of persons containing over two thousand names. All dates have been given as they are found in the original records without change, except that in dates prior to 1753, when the Old Style was in use, the year has been made to correspond with the present calendar, but not the day of the month. This is made necessary by the fact that until 1753 the English people began the year on what was known as *Lady Day*, or March 25th.

There have been so many sources of information that only in a few cases has reference to them been possible. Public records, church records, tombstone inscriptions, newspaper clippings, and family Bibles and other private records, have furnished considerable material. The records of the Friends' Monthly Meetings at Shrewsbury and Burlington, N. J., and Flushing, L. I., and the American Loyalists Manuscripts have been consulted in manuscript form. In addition the chief published authorities and records which have been used are as follows: New Jersey Archives, New York Marriages, New York Colonial Documents, Stillwell's Historical and Genealogical Miscellany, vols. 1 and 2, Salter and Beekman's Old Times in Old Monmouth, Beekman's Early Dutch Settlers of Monmouth County, Symmes' History of Old Tennent Church, Ellis' History of Monmouth County, Salter's History of Monmouth and Ocean Counties, Woodward and Hageman's History of Burlington and Mercer Counties, New Jersey Coast in Three Centuries, vol. 2, Smith's History of New Jersey, Flint's Early Long Island, Bergen's Long Island Families, Hotten's Lists of Emigrants to America, Stryker's Official Register of the Officers and Men of New Jersey in the Revolutionary War, Cooley's Genealogy of Early Settlers in Trenton and Ewing, Burke's Commoners and Landed Gentry. Besides some of the above, the following additional authorities have been consulted for the history of the Throckmorton family, which has involved an amount of work out of all proportion to the size of the sketch in this book: Middletown Town Book, Abstracts of Wills in New York Historical Society's Collections, Rhode Island Colonial Records, Vital Record of Rhode Island, Town Records of Salem (Mass.), Felt's Annals of Salem (Mass.), Brodhead's History of the State of New York, Bolton's History of Westchester County, N. Y., Scharf's History of Westchester County, N. Y., Farmer's Genealogical Record of the First Settlers of New England, Savage's Genealogical Dictionary of New England, Austin's Genealogical Dictionary of Rhode Island, Dictionary of National Biography (British), Burke's Peerage and Baronetage. For two of the family sketches I have also been indebted to the following: The Twining Family (Rev. Ed., 1905), Bergen's VanBrunt Family, and Beekman's A Branch of the VanBrunt Family in Monmouth County (article in N. Y. Gen. and Biog. Record, January and April, 1904.)

This compilation would not have been possible without the aid of many persons who have furnished information for this work. While most of these can not be mentioned, my thanks are especially due to the Rev. William White Hance, James Steen, Esq., and the Hon. George Crawford Beekman, who have given considerable material from their rich stores of genealogical information and who have helped in many other ways. Dr. John E. Stillwell, who has rendered invaluable service in the discovery and preservation of original records, allowed me the privilege of looking over his manuscript notes on the Throckmorton family, and has thus contributed to the accuracy and completeness of the sketch contained in this work. Many excellent suggestions as to the form of these pages have been given by Mr. John H. Cook, and their correctness is in large measure due to his careful supervision in seeing them through the press. To these and to all who have in any way helped, the compiler of these records expresses his grateful appreciation.

ARTHUR S. COLE.

Manasquan, N. J., June 1st, 1908.

CONTENTS.

NOTATION.

In this book every person born in the Scott family is numbered with a separate Arabic numeral. Brothers and sisters in each family are numbered consecutively beginning with a new decade, or, in other words, with the first number of a new group of ten. An asterisk (*) after a personal numeral indicates that the person is a parent, that the numeral is also the number of a family, and that a fuller record of the parents with a list of their children will be found under this number in its regular order. Hence these nnmbers serve the threefold purpose of a personal numeral, a family number, and of indicating the order in the family so far as that is known. An Arabic numeral in brackets [ ] following a name is the personal number, and is thus used in a subsequent (or prior) reference to indicate the exact person mentioned. A superior Arabic numeral (a small figure above the line) after the first name denotes the generation, beginning with the children of William Scott and Abigail Tilton Warner as the first generation. Numbers and small letters in parentheses ( ) are used in the sketches of related families for purposes of numbering and reference.

ILLUSTRATIONS.

FACING PAGE

WILLIAM SCOTT, m. 1679 ABIGAIL TILTON WARNER.

1. JOHN SCOTT, m. MARY BILLS.

- —11. Esther Scott, m. George Crawford.
  - 51. George Crawford.
  - 52. Richard Crawford, m. Catherine Shepherd.
    - 61. Richard Crawford, m. Rebecca Stillwell.
    - 62. George Crawford, m. 1st Mary Seabrook; m. 2d Eleanor Schenck.
    - 63. Catherine Crawford, m. Nathaniel Leonard.
    - 64. Esther Crawford, m. Thomas Burrows.
    - 65. Hannah Crawford, m. Timothy White.
  - 53. William Crawford, m. Catherine Bowne.
    - 301. John Crawford, m. Caroline Fields.
    - 302. William Crawford, m. Rebecca Patterson.
    - 303. Esther Crawford, m. Robert White.
  - 54. Job Crawford, m. Ann Morris.
    - 481. Joshua Crawford.
    - 482. George Crawford.
  - 55. Joshua Crawford.
  - 56. Lydia Crawford, m. 1st Cornelius Compton. m. 2d Benjamin Morris.
    - 491. ——— Compton.
    - 492. ——— Compton.
    - 493. Benjamin Morris, m. ———.
    - 494. Joseph Morris, m. Patience (Herbert?)
    - 495. Stout Morris.
    - 496. Lydia Morris, m. James Frost.
    - 497. Esther Morris, m. Jonathan Stout.
  - 57. Elizabeth Crawford.
- —12. Abigail Scott.
- —13. Mehitable Scott, m. Abraham White.
  - 501. John White, m. 1st Catherine Olden. m. 2d Mary Smith.
    - 511. Job White.
    - 512. Nancy White.
    - 513. James White, m. Martha Hendrickson.
    - 514. Catherine White, m. Giles W. Olden.
    - 515. Benjamin C. White, m. Ann Paxson.
    - 516. Jonathan White.
- —14. William Scott.
- —15. William Scott, m. Mary Runnels.
  - 601. Richard Scott, m. Mary Story.
    - 611. John Scott, m. Mary Schenck.
  - 602. John Scott, m. Sarah Hisson.
    - 621. William Scott, m. Jane Throckmorton.
    - 622. James Scott, m. Ann VanBrunt.
    - 623. Ralph Scott, m. Isabella (Rue?)
    - 624. Sarah Scott, m. James Bennett.
    - 625. Mary Scott, m. Joseph Tilton.
    - 626. Catherin Scott, m. 1st Daniel Hulett; m. 2d Timothy White.
  - 603. George Scott, m. ——.
    - 1271. John W. Scott.
  - 604. Job Scott, m. twice.
    - 1281. Job Scott.
    - 1282. Sarah Scott, m. ——— Woodward.
    - 1283. Ann Scott, m. Daniel Atchley.
  - 605. Ralph Warner Scott.
  - 606. Susannah Scott.
  - 607. Hannah Scott.
    - ? ——. James Reid.
    - ——. William Reid.
    - ——. Eleanor Reid.
  - 608. Sarah Scott, m. David Tilton.
    - 1331. William Tilton, m. Margaret Corlies.
    - 1332. David Tilton, m. (Sarah Flemnen ?)
- —16. Mary Scott, m. 2d John White.
  - 1401. Job White.
  - 1402. Hannah White, m. Garret Covenhoven.
  - 1403. Sarah White, m. ——— Gasper.
  - 1404. Catherine White, m. Samuel Scott.
    - 2781. Aaron Scott.
    - 2782. Jesse Scott.
  - 1405. Aaron White, m. Deborah Trafford.
- —17. Samuel Scott, m. 1st Amy Borden.
  - 1501. Elizabeth Scott, m. Edmund Lafetra.
    - 1511. Edmund Lafetra.
    - 1512. Hannah Lafetra, m. John Pintard.
    - 1513. Amy Lafetra.
    - 1514. Elizabeth Lafetra, m. Daniel Allen.
  - 1502. Hannah Scott, m. William Pintard.
    - 1541. Samuel Pintard, m. Deborah Wall.
    - 1542. Amy Pintard, m. ——— Millet.
    - 1543. Glencross Pintard, m. Catherine Slocum.
    - 1544. Ann Pintard.
    - 1545. William Pintard, m. Lydia Holmes.
    - 1546. John Pintard, m. Hannah Lafetra.
    - 1547. Hannah Pintard, m. Samuel Tilton.
  - 1503. Ebenezer Scott, m. Elizabeth ———.
    - 1651. Samuel Scott, m. Elizabeth Tilton.
    - 1652. Ann Scott, m. John Mount.
  - 1504. John Scott.
  - 1505. Jane Scott.
  - 1506. Amy Scott.
  - 1507. William Scott, m. Ann ———.
- —18. Hannah Scott, m. John Williams.
- —19. John Scott, m. Ruth Stockton.
  - 1901. Samuel Scott.
  - 1902. Richard Scott, m. Lydia ———.
    - 1911. Susannah Scott.
    - 1912. Job Scott, m. ———.
    - 1913. Mehitable Scott.
  - 1903. ? Mehitable Scott, m. John Melrose.
- —20. Ebenezer Scott.
- —21. Ebenezer Scott, m. Patience Leonard.
  - 2201. James Scott, m. Margaret VanCleaf.
    - 2211. William Scott.
    - 2212. Lenah Scott.
    - 2213. Hannah Scott, m. James VanKirk.
    - 2214. Patience Scott, m. 1st Peter H. Conover; m. 2d Garrett Wyckoff.
    - 2215. Sarah Scott.
    - 2216. Ebenezer Scott, m. 1st Eliza Thompson. m. 2d Ann Knott Little.
    - 2217. Benjamin Scott.
    - 2218. Deborah Scott, m. William Little.
    - 2219. James Scott.
  - 2202. Rachel Scott, m. Lewis Conover.
    - 2351. Joseph Conover.
    - 2352. Ebenezer Conover, m. Mary Lefferson.
    - 2353. Hannah Conover.
    - 2354. Mary Conover.
    - 2355. Patience Conover.
    - 2356. Deborah Conover.
    - 2357. Anne Conover.
    - 2358. Helena Conover.
  - 2203. Samuel Scott, m. Catherine White.
    - 2781. Aaron Scott.
    - 2782. Jesse Scott.
  - 2204. William Scott, m. ———.
    - 2791. Samuel Scott.
    - 2792. John Scott.

The Scott Family of Shrewsbury.

INTRODUCTION.

The Scott family of Shrewsbury, N. J., are the descendants of William Scott, the first of the family to settle in Shrewsbury, and his wife, Abigail Tilton Warner. So far as this record is concerned, however, the family story is followed only in the line of William Scott's oldest son, John Scott. William Scott was a Quaker, and probably of English parentage. Family tradition insists upon a Scottish origin, but this is probably based on nothing more than the family name of Scott. This only tells us that the family is of Scotch descent, but does not inform us how far back we must go to find ancestors who lived in Scotland. Martin B. Scott, in his discussion of the "Antiquity of the Name of Scott," says: "The theory of Professor Innes of Edinburgh University, in relation to the original name of Scott in Scotland, is that long before surnames were known, the people of that country, who wandered into England, there received the distinctive appellation of Scotus or Scot, and returned to Scotland bearing the name of Scot in addition to their former name." This is equally true of those who never returned to Scotland, and accounts for the origin of English families of the name of Scott. Another writer says: "The name of Scott ranks among the most prominent British surnames, nearly sixty coats of arms being assigned to it in the Herald's College, and Burke gives the arms of 94 of the name, while the London directory shows about 200 merchants, traders and bankers of this name in that metropolis." However near or remote his Scotch ancestry may have been, we only know that William Scott came to Shrewsbury from Gravesend, Long Island, which was settled by English families.

The compiler of these records has in his possession a book about the size of an old-fashioned family Bible, which has descended to him as an heirloom in the family. It has been known in the family as the "Old Quaker Bible." It is not, however, a Bible, but the famous "Apology for Quakers" by Robert Barclay, and was published in London in 1691. On some of the blank pages are family records, the oldest being the records of the births of the children of William Scott and those of his son John Scott. This book was undoubtedly the property of William Scott, the first of the name to make his home in Shrewsbury, and has been in the possession of the family ever since, for over two hundred years.

There were other persons or families of the name of Scott that settled in New Jersey prior to the Revolutionary War, but it is not known that any of these is related to the others, though further research may reveal relationship in some cases. The list here given does not pretend to be complete, but includes all that a not very thorough search has revealed. Some of these probably never married or had no children:

(1) John Scott of Hanover, Morris county, probably died in 1800, married Sarah, widow of John Budd, Esq.; she died 1780, and had one son by her second husband, John Budd Scott, who married and had two sons, Daniel and John.

(2) Alexander Scott of Elizabeth Town, planter, died 1700, probably son of John Scott who came from Hartford, Conn., about 1660, to Northampton, L. I.; married Ellen———. Issue: Elizabeth, Alexander, Samuel.

(3) David Scott of Somerset county, who on August 18th, 1735, took out a license to marry Jane Canady of Somerset county.

(4) William Scott of Somerset county, died 1797, whose estate was administered by Moses Scott. He was probably some relative of Dr. Moses Scott of New Brunswick. Dr. Moses Scott, died 1822, was a surgeon in the Revolutionary War, a judge of Somerset county 1783-84, and practised medicine in New Brunswick. He married Anna Crane, died 1827, daughter of Elihu and Mary Crane, and had issue: Joseph Warren, Hannah, Jane M., Mary D., Phebe, Margaret, Anna I., Elizabeth.

(5) Robert Scott of Middletown, died intestate 1735.

(6) A family by this name seems to have settled very early in Cumberland county, for Abigail, Hannah, Mary, Ruth and Sidnea Scott married in this county at dates ranging from 1770 to 1789.

(7) Timothy Scott of Salem county, died about 1747, probably married Sarah———.

(8) William Scott of Penn's Neck, Salem county, died 1759, married Susanna———. Issue: William, John, Anne, Mary, Elizabeth, Susanna, Robert, Joseph.

(9) Robert Scott of Greenwich Township, Gloucester county, died 1779, son of John Scott of near Londonderry, Ireland; married Margaret———. He left part of his estate to his brother William in Ireland, who may have subsequently immigrated to this country.

(10) Henry Scott of Burlington, born 1664, died 1714, son of Jonathan Scott of near Edenderry, Kings County, Ireland; married 1698 Ann Wright, daughter of Thomas Wright. Issue: Thomas, Henry, Abraham, Jonathan, John, Mary.

(11) Joseph Scott of Chesterfield Township, Burlington county, forge carpenter, died 1726.

(12) James Scott of Mansfield, Burlington county, mariner, died 1730.

(13) Benjamin Scott of Burlington, died May 9th, 1684, married 1st, Margaret———, who died December 26th, 1682; married 2d, February 12th, 1684, Mrs. Hannah Kimball, a widow, died October 16th, 1697, the daughter of "John Chaffon, of Burlington county, gentleman." Issue, all by first marriage: Benjamin, John, Margaret, Bridget, Martin, Elizabeth. Benjamin Scott was one of the founders and first settlers of Burlington, N. J., in 1677, being one of the commissioners of the London Quakers. He came from Widdington, County of Essex, England, and was probably the son of William Scott, as William Scott junior is mentioned as his brother in a deed. He has been supposed to be a brother of William Scott of Shrewsbury, and its improbability is discussed elsewhere. In the "New Jersey Coast in Three Centuries," it is stated that Benjamin Scott was the grandson of Richard Scott (born 1544, died 1628), a member of the house of Buccleuch, who came from Scotland and settled at Shrewsbury in Shropshire, England, becoming there the founder of the Scotts of Betton. He is thus identified with the Benjamin Scott who was baptized September 20th, 1631, and who married Susannah Brerewood and went to Barbadoes. Authority for this identification is lacking, and Benjamin Scott of Burlington came from

Widdington, England, not from Barbadoes. Further, in a census of the Island of Barbadoes taken in 1679 and 1680, Benjamin Scott is recorded as having 108 acres of land, 2 white servants and 41 negroes in the Parish of Christ Church, and 10 acres of land in the Parish of St. Michaels, which seems to show that he was not the same person whose home and family were at the same time in Burlington in the Province of West Jersey. In Woodward and Hageman's "History of Burlington and Mercer Counties, N. J.," it is claimed that one of the families of Burlington owning the name of Scott is descended from Benjamin Scott through his son Henry, and still owns part of the original land. But Benjamin Scott had no son by the name of Henry, so far as any record shows, and the Henry Scott who lived in Burlington was of an entirely different family, being the son of Jonathan Scott, of near Edenderry in Kings county, Ireland, as shown by an advertisement in the *Pennsylvania Gazette* of June 15th, 1758.

I.

William Scott and Abigail Tilton Warner.

The first certain record that we have of William Scott's presence in this country is in the "New York Marriages," where we find that he took out a license to marry Abigail Warner February 7th, 1678, which would be 1679 according to our modern way of dating the year to begin January 1st, instead of March 25th, as was customary in Great Britain and her colonies before 1753. At the time of his marriage William Scott resided at Gravesend, Long Island. The records of this town show that on May 31st, 1660, one of this name bought of Nicholas Stillwell a house and garden in Gravesend, signing his name "William Scot." If this was the same William Scott, and it seems probable, he must have been born not later than the year 1639, and was thus considerably older than his wife, Abigail Tilton Warner, who was born in 1650. She was the daughter of John and Mary Tilton of Gravesend, and widow of Ralph Warner of Barbadoes. Her first husband, Ralph Warner, marriage license dated May 15th, 1669, died at Barbadoes, and was buried there, according to the parish register of St. Michael's church, April 24th, 1678. There were two children by this first marriage, Mary Warner, born at New Utrecht, L. I., and Ralph Warner, born at Brookland, L. I., June, 167—. The latter died at Shrewsbury, N. J., in 1695, probably in July. The following is from the records of the Court of Sessions of the West Riding of Yorkshire, Long Island, at the Court held at Gravesend, beginning December 18th, 1678: "Upon the Peticon of Abigail Warner wherein shee desires to be freed from the paymt of her deceased Husbands Debts, shee being left in a desolate, and poor condicon by her said Husband, and nothing considerable left her for the paymt thereof and for the subsistance, and maintainance of her selfe, & children, There being an Inventory brought into the cort of what was left by her said Husband, not amounting to more than the Value of 40s. The cort allowes the same, and Order yt shee shall not be lyable thereunto, having so inconsiderable a pt of her Husbands Estate for the maintenance of her selfe, & children."

William Scott removed his family and settled at Shrewsbury, N. J., in 1682 or 1683. His home here was in that part of Shrewsbury township bordering on Swimming River, near Newman's Spring. Two patents, both for land in Shrewsbury, are on record. One, dated March 25th, 1688, is for 140 acres on Ramsonts Neck, the right to which he had purchased from Peter Tilton, probably on his first settlement in the county, for Peter Tilton had taken out a patent for these and other lands as early as 1681. This land is briefly described as follows: "136 acres, N. Naversinks R., E. John Slocume, W. and S. roads, and 4 acres of meadow on Racoone Neck, W. Nicholas Broun, E. John Burdein, N. Narawataconck R., S. upland." The four acres on Raco Island, or Racoone Neck, were sold to Hannanias Giffard December 10th, 1684. The other patent, dated March 22d, 1688, is for land for which a Governor's warrant had been

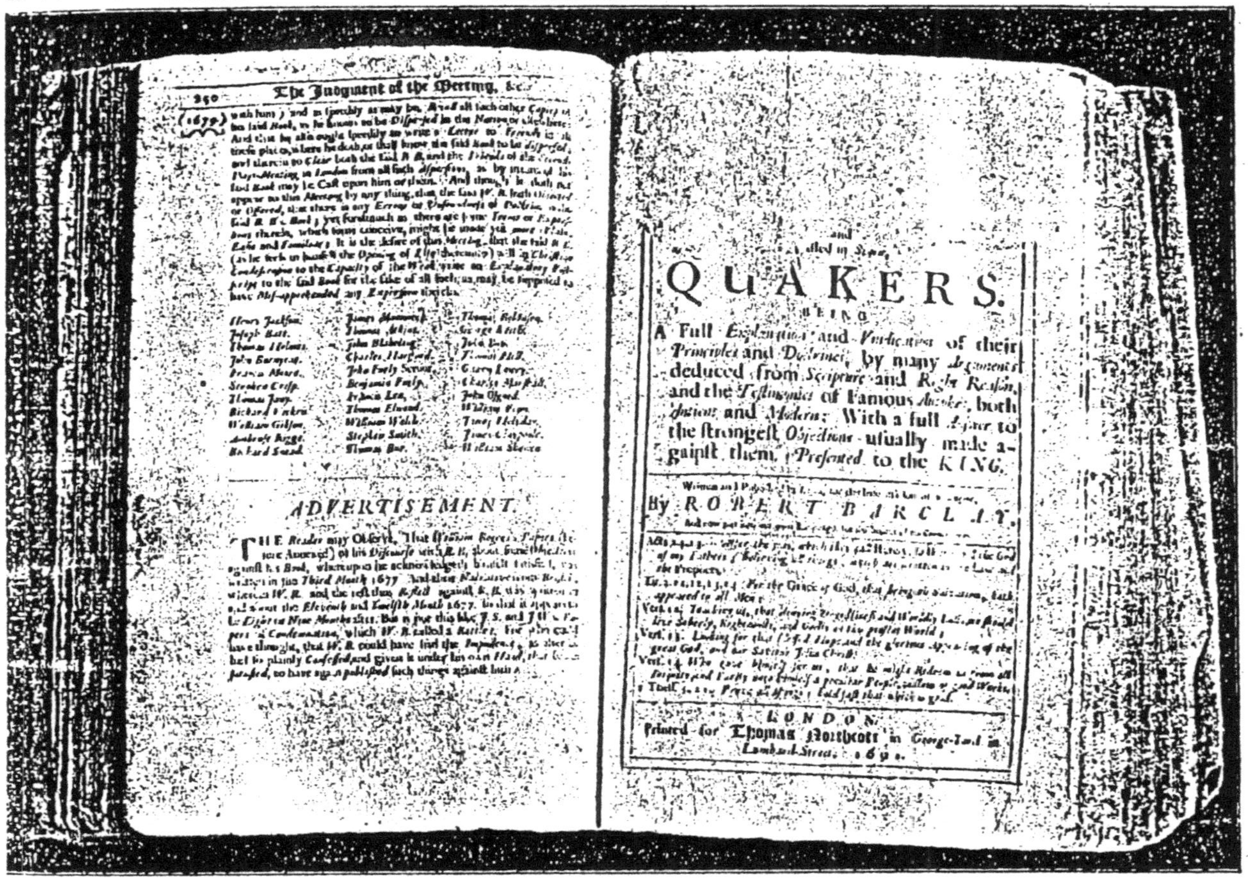

Barclay's "Apology for Quakers" which has been in the family over 200 years.
For the oldest birth records found in this book, see illustration facing page 54.

taken out December 16th, 1685. This land is described as follows: "145 acres at Passequenecqua, E. the creek, W. the Proprietors, N. Restore Leppencott, S. Nathaniel Slocume, also 5½ acres of meadow, N. and S. upland, E. John Leppencott, W. Nathl Slocume." William Scott was a farmer by occupation, and a Quaker in religious belief. His name occurs frequently in the records of the Friends' Monthly Meeting of Shrewsbury. On the occasion of a marriage on the 9th day of the 11th month, 1689 (January 9th, 1690), the names of both William Scott and William Scott, Jr., are signed as witnesses. One of these names cannot be that of a son, for both sons of this name died in infancy. If some other relative, it is the only record we have of his presence here or anywhere else in the colony. William Scott was a grand juror in 1692, and was still living in 1699, in which year sickness or infirmity made him too weak to sign his own name to a deed. He must have died soon after, certainly prior to 1707. He had children as follows:

1*. JOHN[1] SCOTT, born January 9th, 1680, at Gravesend, married Mary Bills.

2. WILLIAM[1] SCOTT, born October 8th, 1681, at Gravesend, died "ye later end of ye 10 mo." (December), 1682, probably at Shrewsbury.

3. WILLIAM[1] SCOTT, born December 25th, 1683, at Shrewsbury, died January 8th, 1684, at Shrewsbury.

4. SAMUEL[1] SCOTT, born May 31st, 1685, at Shrewsbury; nothing more is known about him.

5. PETER[1] SCOTT, born September 27th, 1687, at Shrewsbury, died October 2d, 1687, at Shrewsbury.

6. ESTHER[1] SCOTT, born December 6th, 1689, at Shrewsbury; nothing more is known about her.

WILLIAM SCOTT'S ANCESTRY.

Where was William Scott born? What were his family connections? When did he or his family come to America? Though remotely of Scottish ancestry and probably of English parentage, no positive answers can be given to these questions. In the account of the Scott family given in "New Jersey Coast in Three Centuries," volume ii., pages 166-168, nearly every statement of which is incorrect, it is claimed that William Scott of Shrewsbury was the brother of Benjamin Scott of Burlington, and thus came to America in 1677 from Widdington, county of Essex, not far from London, England. This is based upon two deeds, of which the following descriptions are taken from the "New Jersey Archives:"

(1) "April 3d, 1677. Deed. John Kinsey, late of Great Hadham, Co. of Hertford, England, gent: to Benjamin Scott and William Scott junior, both of Widdington, Co. of Essex, husbandmen, for ⅓ of a share of W. J."

(2) "Nov. 7th, 1691. Deed. John Scott to James Bingham, both of Burlington Co., yeomen, for 200 acres bo't of his father Benjamin Scott and Uncle William Scott April 3d, 1677."

Benjamin Scott was one of the commissioners of the London Quakers who, together with some Quakers from Yorkshire, founded Burlington, N. J., in 1677. On their way here they had first anchored at Sandy Hook, and their presence in New York is confirmed by a council minute dated August 4th, 1677. William Scott may well have left the ship here and settled at Gravesend, L. I., for his name does not appear among the settlers at Burlington. But there is not sufficient evidence to identify the William Scott junior of these deeds with the William Scott of Gravesend, and other evidence seems to contradict it.

William Scott appears to have been in Gravesend earlier than 1677, and probably belonged to the family of this name that had resided here almost from the beginning of the settlement. A Rodger Scott is mentioned among the settlers of Gravesend in December, 1646, and in that year he was given a plantation lot. He is probably the same as the Roger Scott who in 1642 was in Lynn, Mass., the town from which came many of the first settlers of Gravesend. He sold some land in September, 1647, and in 1651 leased house and land in Gravesend from one Randell Scott and sublet the same to William Oliver. William Scott bought a house and garden in Gravesend from Nicholas Stillwell, May 31st, 1660. On January 11th, 1681, Lourens Jurianse bought from Denyse Theunissen of Flushing a house and garden in Gravesend which had lately been occupied by William Scott. Whether Rodger Scott was the father of William Scott, or whether they were related at all, it is impossible to say. It it hoped that further investigations will reveal other records that may throw some light upon the parentage and ancestry of William Scott, and thus make a revision of this ancestral history necessary.

THE TILTON FAMILY.

John and Mary Tilton, the parents of Abigail Tilton, who became the wife of William Scott, were residents of Lynn, Mass., as early as 1640. From the Lynn records of the date of December 14th, 1642, we read: "Lady Deborah Moodie, Mrs. King and the wife of John Tilton were presented for houlding that the baptism of infants is not ordained of God." "The proceedings against them resulted in their leaving Lynn, and the next year (1643), we find mention of Lady Moodie, the Tiltons, William Goulding, Samuel Spicer and others at Gravesend, Long Island, founding the settlement from which afterward came many persons to Old Monmouth." John Tilton was town clerk of Gravesend in 1654-56. After the appearance of the Quakers here in 1657, he and his wife seem to have joined with them, for from this time they were often fined and persecuted for helping the Quakers. In 1658 John Tilton was imprisoned on the charge of the Schout of Gravesend that he had lodged a Quakeress, for which offense he was fined £12 Flemish money, a sum equivalent to $28.80, and costs. In 1662 he was fined again "for permitting Quakers to quake" at his house. "On the 5th of Oct., 1662, John Tilton and Mary his wife were summoned before the Governor and his council, at New Amsterdam, charged with having entertained Quakers and frequenting their conventicles. They were condemned and ordered to leave the province before the 20th of Nov. following, under pain of corporal punishment." It is supposed that this sentence was reversed or changed to a fine. From the record of the trial we read: "Goody Tilton (Mrs. Tilton) was not so much condemmed for assisting at conventicles as for having, like a sorceress, gone from door to door to lure and seduce the people, yea even young girls, to join the Quakers."—*Old Times in Old Monmouth*, p. 145f.

John Tilton died at Gravesend in 1688. His will, dated September 15th, 1687, was recorded April 3d, 1688. His wife died May 29, 1683. Their children were as follows:

(1) John Tilton, born June 4th, 1640, married 1st, Mary Coats, and 2d, Rebecca Terry. Issue by second wife: Abraham, Samuel, Sarah, Daniel, Thomas, Mary, Hester.

(2) Peter Tilton, born January, 1643, married April 22d, 1665, Rebecca Brazier, daughter of Henry Brazier.

(3) Sarah Tilton, born May 4th, 1644, married John Painter.

(4) Esther Tilton, born 1647, died 1703, married 1665, Samuel Spicer, died 1692, son of Thomas and Michal Spicer. Issue: Jacob, Mary, Sarah, Martha, Sarah, Abigail.

(5) Abigail Tilton, born 1650, married 1st, 1669, Ralph Warner, and 2d, 1679, William Scott.

(6) Thomas Tilton, born March 1st, 1652.

(7) Mary Tilton, born June, 1654, married Henry Boman.

II.

John Scott and Mary Bills.

1. JOHN[1] SCOTT, born January 9th, 1680, at Gravesend, L. I., died 1736, married about 1700 Mary Bills, born April 14th, 1679, at Eastham, Mass., daughter of Thomas Bills and Joanna Twining. He resided on the homestead farm inherited from his father near Newman's Spring. He was a grand juror in 1711. He had eleven children, as follows:

11*. ESTHER[2] SCOTT, born May 13th, 1701, married George Crawford.

12. ABIGAIL[2] SCOTT, born February 5th, 1704, probably died young.

13*. MEHITABLE[2] SCOTT, born January 16th, 1707, married Abraham White.

14. WILLIAM[2] SCOTT, born August 16th, 1709, died in infancy.

15*. WILLIAM[2] SCOTT, a twin, born August 30th, 1712, married Mary Runnels.

16*. MARY[2] SCOTT, a twin, born August 30th, 1712, married 1st Thomas Tollet and 2d John White.

17*. SAMUEL[2] SCOTT, born August 11th, 1715, married 1st Amy Borden and 2d Sarah Allen.

18. HANNAH[2] SCOTT, born December 19th, 1717. She is possibly the one who married John Williams of Shrewsbury as his second wife, marriage license dated July 18th, 1751. There appear to have been no children by this marriage, but in his will (Trenton Wills, L. 424) John Williams (died 1776) mentions Rachel Scott, "whom I have brought up." She is undoubtedly the Rachel Scott who married in 1771 George Gardner, but if she has any place in the family it has not been ascertained.

19*. JOHN[2] SCOTT, born November 3d, 1719, married Ruth Stockton.

20. EBENEZER[2] SCOTT, born November 10th, or 19th, 1721, died in infancy.

21*. EBENEZER[2] SCOTT, born May 17th, 1723, married Patience Leonard.

THE WILL OF JOHN SCOTT.

IN THE NAME OF GOD AMEN the therteenth day of September in the Year of Our Lord One thousand Seven hundred and thirty Six I John Scott of Shrewsbury in the County of Monmouth and Province of East New Jersey Planter being very Sick and weak in Body but of perfect Mind and memory thanks be given to God therefore Calling to mind the mortality of my Body and knowing thatt itt is appointed for Man once to Die do Make and Ordain this my last Will and Testament thatt is to say principally and first of all I Give and Recommend my Soul into the hands of God thatt gave it and my Body I recommend itt to the Earth to be buried in a Christian like and devout manner at the discretion of my Executors nothing Doubting butt att the General Resurrection I shall recieve the same again by the mighty Power of God and as touching sutch Worldly Estate wherewith it hath pleased God to bless me in this life I Give Devise and dispose of the same in the following manner and fform Viz: IMPRIMIS it is my Will and I do Order thatt in the first Place all my Just Debts and ffuneral Charges be Paid and satisfied ITEM I Give and Bequeath unto my Eldest Son William all that Tract of Land to the Southward of my Plantation formerly belonging to Abraham Vickers with the House and Appurtenasses thereunto belonging Beginning att a Chesnutt Tree mark'd near Newmans Spring on the Bank of the River and from thence Eastwardly to within two Rods of George Allens Corner and thence further to a Wallnutt Saplin marked on three sides near the Corner of a ffield thence due East to Edmond Lefetras Land To Gether with my uper peace of meddow known by the name of Glass makers Landing ITEM I Give to my Second Son Samuel thatt Tract of Land to the North ward of my Plantation together with the House and and Appurtenances thereunto belonging for him his Heirs and Assigns for Ever Beginning at the River thence up a Gully to a Red Oake Tree marked on the three Sides East. thence South Easterly to the North West Corner of the Old Peach Orchard thence East to the highway Together with my lower meddow ITEM I give to my Son William the one half of my homestid being the remainder of my Plantation to be Devided both in Quantity and Quality upon then Consideration of his paying to my Son John the full and Just Sum of One hundred and twenty five pounds att his Arrival at the Age of twenty one Years and if William neglects the Payment of said Sum of money then the said part of the Plantation shall belong to John his heirs and Assigns to have and to hold for Ever ITEM I give to my Son Samuell the other half of Homestid both in quantity and Quality upon the Consideration of his paying to my Son Ebenezer the full and Just Sum of One hundred and twenty five Pounds att his Arrival to the Age of twenty one Years and if Samuell neglects the Payment of said Sum of money then the said part of the Plantation shall belong to Ebenezer his heirs and Assigns to have and to hold for Ever ITEM my Will is that if either John or Ebenezer shall Dye before they Cum to Age and leave no lawfull Issue the Survivor shall have the whole Part or homestid hee his heirs or Assigns to have & to hold for Ever ITEM I give to my daughter Mercy Tollet one Bed and Beding two Cowes One Horse likewise my will is thatt She shall have her Abode in my dwelling House till the time that my Youngest Son Ebenezer be of the Age of twenty One and the privalidge of keeping her Cretures and of Hay for them ITEM I give to my Daughter Hannah one Bed and Beding two Cowes and One Horse likewise her living in my Dwelling House as long as She remains Single and the Priviledge of Keeping her Cretures and of Hay for them—And the Orchards my Will is thatt thay be maid Use of betwen my two Sons William and Samuel and my two Daughters Mercy and Hannah untill my Son Ebenezer Cums of Age or my Son John ITEM I give the Use of the homestid otherwise & then whatt is before mentioned to my Sons William and Samuel upon Condition thatt they keep itt in good Fence and repare and Soe butt one peace in four Year untill the time that my Son John is of Age and likewise to Repare the dwelling House and Barn ITEM my Will is that the Negro Gerl Johannah live with my Daughter Mehethabel White until She be one and twenty Years of Age and the to return to the Estate ITEM my Will is that after my Debts are payd the remainder of my Movebels shall be Devided equaly among all my Children ITEM I do hereby likewise Constitute make Ordain and Appointt my two Sons William and Samuel Scott with my Son in Law George Crawford the Executors of this my last Will and Testament And I do hereby utterly Dissalow Revoke and Disanul all and every other former Testaments Wills Legacies and Executors by Mee in any way before this Time Named Willed and bequeathed, Ratifing and Conferning this and nother to be my last Will and Testament IN WITNESS whereof I have hereunto Sett my Hand and Seal the Day and Year above written.

JOHN SCOTT. [L. S.]

Signed Sealed published pronounced and Declared by the said John Scott as his last Will and Testament in the presence of Us the Subscribers William Leeds James Grover John H (his mark) Hanskins John White Christopher Nicholson.

This will (Trenton Wills, C, 128) was proved November 17th, 1736, with executors as named.

THE BILLS FAMILY.

Thomas Bills, the father of Mary Bills who became the wife of John Scott [1], was probably the son of William Bills, one of the first settlers of Barnstable, Mass., in 1640. He married 1st October 3d, 1672, Anna Twining, the daughter of William Twining and Elizabeth Deane, who died September 1st, 1675. He married 2d May 2d, 1676, Joanna Twining, a sister of his first wife, who died June 4th, 1723. He lived at Eastham, Mass., but removed to Yarmouth, and from there to Burlington, N. J., not later than 1695, probably in that year. He did not stay in Burlington long, for we find his wife's name as a witness at a marriage at Shrewsbury in March, and his own in May, 1696. He seems to have lived for a while, however, at Woodbridge, as the following description of a lease from the "New Jersey Archives" shows: "February 19th, 1696-7. Lease. Mary, widow of Thomas Carhart of Woodbridge, to Thomas Bills of Burlington, West Jersey, weaver, for a house and farm on Craine Cr., Woodbridge, 120 acres; lease ended by mutual consent June 11th, 1698." He then took up his permanent residence in Shrewsbury, for we read again in the "New Jersey Archives": "September 16th, 1701. Deed. Thomas Bills of Shrewsbury, weaver, to his son-in-law David Killie of Middletown, for one half of the lot on the N. side of Sawmill Brook, W. another brook." Thomas Bills died at Shrewsbury April 2d, 1721. He had the following children, most of them, if not all, born at Eastham, Mass., and all but the first two by his second wife:

(1) Anne Bills, born June 26th, or 28th, 1673, married 1692 David Killie, son of David and Jane Killie.

(2) Elizabeth Bills, born August 23d, 1675.

(3) Nathaniel Bills, born June 25th, 1677, died 1729 at Shrewsbury. His will, dated January 24th, 1729, proved March 31st, 1729, names the following children: Thomas, Gershom, Daniel (under age), Marcey, Catherine, Joanna and Elizabeth.

(4) Mary, or Mercy, Bills, born April 14th, 1679, married John Scott [1*].

(5) Mehitable Bills, born March 26th, 1681.

(6) Thomas Bills, born March 22d, 1684, died 1729 at Shrewsbury; married 1st Elizabeth Shotwell, and 2d Content Woolley, daughter of Edward Woolley and Lydia Allen, who married 2d May 27th, 1736, Isaac Hance, as his second wife. The will of Thomas Bills, dated February 22d, 1729, proved March 24th, 1729, mentions the following children, all under age: William, Silvanus, Thomas, Joanna, Lydia and Elizabeth.

(7) Gershom Bills, born June 5th, 1686, died 1766, married 2d Margaret Chamberlin, marriage license dated April 7th, 1755, and had nine children.

(8) Joanna Bills, born December 2d, 1688, died April 1st, 1728, married January 27th, 1709 (marginal record, June 11th, 1710), George Williams, son of John Williams and Elizabeth Allen. Issue: Obediah, Hezekiah, George, John and Experience.

THE TWINING FAMILY.

"Mr. William Twining, Sr.," came to Plymouth, Mass., from England, some time between 1630 and 1640. His name is first found in the Plymouth Court Records, June 1st, 1641, in a case of trespass regarding certain lands. He was then a resident of Yarmouth, situated some thirty miles southeast of Plymouth. Records from 1643 to 1645 rank him among the militia, which consisted of fifty soldiers, and in 1645 he was one of five soldiers sent out against the Narragansetts. In 1645, or soon after, he removed to Eastham. Here he married his second wife, Anna Doane, in 1652. She died February 27th, 1680. His death occurred April 15th, 1659, when he was not over seventy years old. So far as known, he had but two children, Isabel and William, and they by his first wife, born prior to his coming to the colony.

Isabel Twining died May 16th, 1706, at Yarmouth. On June 17th, 1641, she married Francis Baker, who was born in Hertfordshire, England, in 1611, came over in the "Planter" in 1635, and died July 23d, 1696. They had the following children: Nathaniel, John, Samuel, Daniel, William, Thomas, Elizabeth and Hannah.

William Twining, Jr., was born about 1625, "probably in England." He is first mentioned in the records when he married about 1650, at Eastham, Elizabeth Deane, the daughter of Stephen Deane and Elizabeth Ring of Plymouth. Stephen Deane was one of the first settlers, coming over in the "Fortune" in 1621, and building the first corn mill in New England in 1632. He married Elizabeth, the daughter of Mrs. Mary Ring, a widow, had three children, Elizabeth, Miriam and Susanna, and died in 1634. William Twining, Jr., was admitted and sworn in 1652. He was four times one of the grand jury from 1652 to 1671. As early as 1677 he was a deacon of the Eastham church, and is alluded to as "Deacon Twining" as late as 1681. Previous to 1695, however, when his name appears on the Eastham records for the last time, he became a Quaker, and this necessitated a change of residence to escape persecution. Therefore we find him and his son Stephen locating in the new province of Pennsylvania, at Newtown, Bucks county. His name first appears in the records of Middletown Friends' Monthly Meeting in 1699, in connection with his son Stephen's, to a testimony against selling rum or strong drink to the Indians. He died November 4th, 1703; his wife died December 28th, 1708. His will, dated June 26th, 1697, was proved April 6th, 1705.

William Twining, Jr., had children as follows:

(1) Elizabeth Twining, died March 10th, 1725, married August 19th, 1669, John Rogers, son of Joseph Rogers, born April 3d, 1642, died January 10th, 1738; lived in Eastham. Issue: Samuel, John, Judah, Joseph, Elizabeth, Mehitable, Eleazar, Hannah, Nathaniel.

(2) Anna Twining, died September 1st, 1675, married October 3d, 1672, Thomas Bills. Issue: Anna, Elizabeth.

(3) Susanna Twining, born January 25th, or February 28th, 1654, died young.

(4) William Twining, born probably same date as Susanna, died January 23d, 1735, married March 21st, 1689, Ruth Cole, daughter of John and Ruth Cole, born 1688, died after 1735. He remained a Puritan and stayed at Eastham. Issue: Elizabeth, Thankful, Ruth, Hannah, William, Barnabas, Mercy.

(5) Mehitable Twining, supposed to have married Daniel Doane, Jr., of Eastham. He and his family came on the overland route in 1696, and settled on land adjoining the Twinings in Newtown, Pa. He deposited a card with the Sandwich Society of Friends with wife Mehitable and children Daniel, Lydia, Rebecca, Elijah, Eleazar and Joseph.

(6) Joanna Twining, born May 30th, 1657, died June 4th, 1723, married May 2d, 1676, Thomas Bills as his second wife. Issue: Nathaniel, Mary or Mercy, Mehitable, Thomas, Gershom, Joanna.

(7) Stephen Twining, born February 6th, 1659, died February 8th, 1720, married January 3d, 1683, Abigail Young, daughter of John and Abigail Young, born 1660, died April 9th, 1715. Issue: Stephen, Eleazar, Nathaniel, Mercy, John.

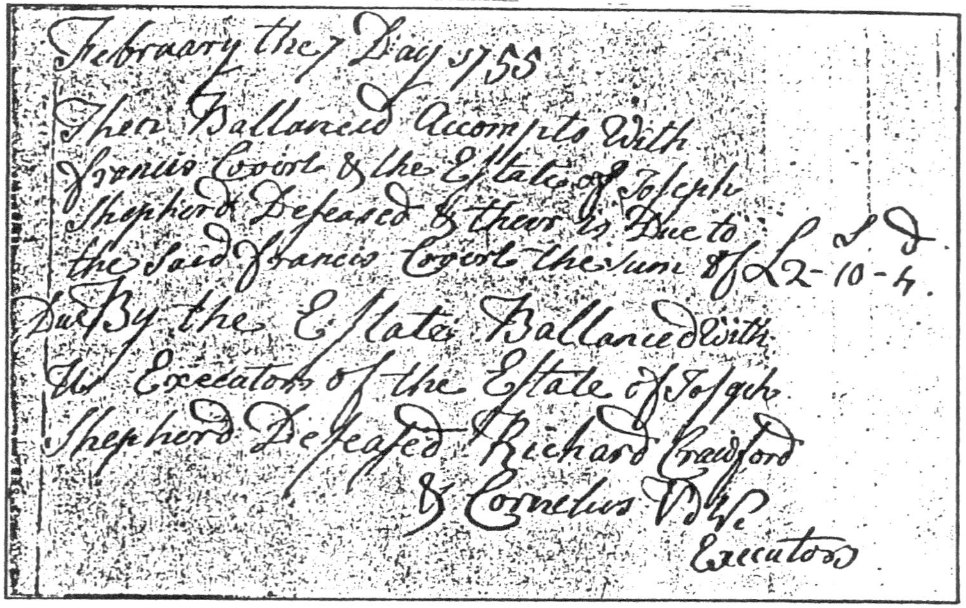

February the 7 Day 1755
Then Ballanced Accompts With
Francis Covert & the Estate of Joseph
Shepherd Deseased & their is Due to s d
the said Francis Covert the sum of £2-10-4.
Due By the Estate Ballanced With
the Executors of the Estate of Joseph
Shepherd Deseased Richard Crawford
& Cornelius Vdye
Executors

Part of a page from an old account book originally belonging to Joseph Shepherd, containing the signature of Richard[3] Crawford [52].

III.

George Crawford and Esther Scott.

11. ESTHER[2] SCOTT, born May 13th, 1701, died later than 1745, daughter of John Scott [1] and Mary Bills, married about 1726 GEORGE CRAWFORD, died 1745, son of John Crawford, Jr., and Abigail his wife. They lived on the old Crawford homestead at Nutswamp in Middletown township, which had been first conveyed to John Crawford by patent from the Proprietors of East Jersey December 3d, 1687 (Trenton Deeds, B, 211). George Crawford's will, dated March 15th, 1745, was proved at Perth Amboy May 10th, 1745, and is recorded at Trenton (D, 279). Issue:

51. GEORGE[3] CRAWFORD, born 1727, died unmarried about 1750.

52*. RICHARD[3] CRAWFORD, born January 27th, 1729, married Catherine Shepherd.

53*. WILLIAM[3] CRAWFORD, married Catherine Bowne.

54*. JOB[3] CRAWFORD, married Ann Morris.

55. JOSHUA[3] CRAWFORD, went South, where he probably has descendants.

56*. LYDIA[3] CRAWFORD, married 1st, license dated July 30th, 1756, Cornelius Compton of Middletown, by whom she is said to have had two sons; married 2d, 1767, Benjamin Morris.

57. ELIZABETH[3] CRAWFORD, born 1745, after her father's death.

---

52. RICHARD[3] CRAWFORD, born January 27th, 1729, died September 20th, 1798, married, license dated September 17th, 1751, Catherine Shepherd, born August 11th, 1734, died January 13th, 1807, daughter of Joseph Shepherd and Rebecca Lippet. They lived on the Crawford homestead farm at Nutswamp. Richard Crawford was prominent in the affairs of the Baptist church at Middletown, and it is on record that in May, 1769, he was chosen to the office of ruling elder in that church. His will, dated October 1st, 1794, was proved March 8th, 1806 (Monmouth Co. Wills, A, 116). Issue:

61*. RICHARD[4] CRAWFORD, born 1756, married Rebecca Stillwell.

62*. GEORGE[4] CRAWFORD, born December 5th, 1758, married 1st Mary Seabrook and 2d Eleanor Schenck.

63*. CATHERINE[4] CRAWFORD, married Nathaniel Leonard.

64*. ESTHER[4] CRAWFORD, married Thomas Burrows.

65*. HANNAH[4] CRAWFORD, married Timothy White.

---

61. RICHARD[4] CRAWFORD, born 1756, died November 12th, 1837, married Rebecca Stillwell; lived on Crawford homestead at Nutswamp. Issue:

71. RICHARD[5] CRAWFORD, died young, unmarried.

72. CATHERINE[5] CRAWFORD, married John Bowne[5] Crawford [361*].

---

62. GEORGE[4] CRAWFORD, born December 5th, 1758, died July 11th, 1834, married 1st Mary Seabrook, born 1766, died January 9th, 1795, daughter of Major Thomas Seabrook and Martha Tallman; married 2d January 27th, 1799, Eleanor Schenck, born March 17th, 1764, died May 17th, 1850, daughter of Hendrick Schenck and Catherine Holmes. He

lived at Middletown, and had five children, all but the first by his second wife. His will, dated July 13th, 1825, was proved July 23d, 1834 (Monmouth Co. Wills, C, 338). Issue:

81. CATHERINE[5] CRAWFORD, born August 12th, 1793, married Edward[5] Burrows [221*].

82*. MARY[5] CRAWFORD, born January 12th, 1800, married William W. Murray.

83*. ANN[5] CRAWFORD, born February 22d, 1801, married Rev. Jacob Ten Broek Beekman.

84*. ADALINE[5] CRAWFORD, born February 16th, 1803, married John Lloyd Hendrickson.

85. ELEANOR[5] CRAWFORD, born January 26th, 1807, died December 22d, 1823.

---

82. MARY[5] CRAWFORD, born January 12th, 1800, died January 17th, 1853, married November 20th, 1817, William W. Murray, born November 30th (or 20th), 1794, died June 1st, 1865, son of William Murray and Anne Schenck; resided at Middletown. Issue:

91. LAVINIA[6] MURRAY, born December 17th, 1818, died 1876, married August 26th, 1847, James M. Hoagland, a merchant of New York City, whom she survived; resided in Jersey City and New York City; no issue.

92*. ELEANOR CRAWFORD[6] MURRAY, born July 21st, 1823, married Henry G. Scudder.

93*. GEORGE CRAWFORD[6] MURRAY, born January 3d, 1827, married Mary Catherine Cooper.

---

92. ELEANOR CRAWFORD[6] MURRAY, born July 21st, 1823, died 1858, married May 1st, 1849, Henry G. Scudder of Huntington, L. I., a descendant of Thomas Scudder, the first immigrant of the name at Salem, Mass., in 1635. Issue:

101. WILLIAM MURRAY[7] SCUDDER, born May 23d, 1850, died young, unmarried.

102. MARY CRAWFORD[7] SCUDDER, born June 29th, 1852, died young, unmarried.

103. NORA JARVIS[7] SCUDDER, born March 30th, 1854, died young, unmarried.

104. HENRY G.[7] SCUDDER, born November 9th, 1856; resides on the Scudder homestead at Huntington, L. I.; unmarried.

---

93. GEORGE CRAWFORD[6] MURRAY, born January 3d, 1827, died November 24th, 1884, married February 27th, 1855, Mary Catherine Cooper, born March 20th, 1833, died 1905, daughter of James Cooper and Rebecca Patterson. He graduated from Yale University in 1845, the youngest member of his class, and studied law in New York City, being admitted to the bar of that state in 1849. In 1851, however, the sickness of his parents, now alone with the care of two large farms, obliged him to return to his home in Middletown. Issue:

111*. MARY CRAWFORD[7] MURRAY, born December 29th, 1855, married Dr. Ovid Allen Hyde.

112*. ELLA COOPER[7] MURRAY, born September 6th, 1857, married William T. VanBrunt.

113*. GEORGE CRAWFORD[7] MURRAY, born April 15th, 1868, married Gertrude Whitman.

---

111. MARY CRAWFORD[7] MURRAY, born December 29th, 1855, married June 11th, 1887, Dr. Ovid Allen Hyde, born July 22d, 1855, and engaged in the practice of medicine in New York City. Issue:

121. CHESTER OVID[8] HYDE, born July 22d, 1888.

122. GEORGE CRAWFORD MURRAY[8] HYDE, born December 23d, 1890, died September 25th, 1891.

---

112. ELLA COOPER[7] MURRAY, born September 6th, 1857, married June 11th, 1889, William T. VanBrunt of Middletown township. Issue:

131. A son[8], died in infancy.

132. CATHERINE ELEANOR[8] VANBRUNT, born September 4th, 1900.

113. GEORGE CRAWFORD[7] MURRAY, born April 15th, 1868, married June 23d,

1897, Gertrude Whitman of Brooklyn, where she died March 3d, 1899; resides in Brooklyn. Issue:

141. GERTRUDE DOROTHY[8] MURRAY, born February 4th, 1899.

---

83. ANN[5] CRAWFORD, born February 22d, 1801, died May 18th, 1876, married February 12th, 1833, Rev. Jacob Ten Broek Beekman, born April 10th, 1801, died April 23d, 1875, son of Captain Samuel Beekman and Helena TenBroek. He was born in the brick farmhouse erected by the Hon. Cornelius Ten Broek prior to the Revolution near Harlingen, Somerset Co., N. J., and which is still standing and in use. He was a graduate of Union College, Schenectady, N. Y., and studied theology at the Reformed (Dutch) Seminary at New Brunswick, N. J. He was licensed to preach in 1826, and was called to the Dutch Reformed Church of Middletown township, near Holmdel, where he remained ten years. Issue:

151. EDWIN[6] BEEKMAN, born November 8th, 1833, died August 12th, 1834.

152. THEODORE[6] BEEKMAN, born January 31st, 1835, died June 22d, 1902.

153. ELEANOR CRAWFORD[6] BEEKMAN, born May 5th, 1836, died March 27th, 1882.

154. MARY[6] BEEKMAN, born August 4th, 1838, died August 19th, 1838.

155*. GEORGE CRAWFORD[6] BEEKMAN, born July 2d, 1839, married Laura B. Alston.

156. EDWIN[6] BEEKMAN, born June 13th, 1842, a farmer, living on the homestead farm in Middletown. He served as journal clerk of the House of Representatives at Washington, D. C., during a part of the Cleveland administration, and was for a number of years clerk of the grand jury of Monmouth County. He has contributed many articles on agricultural matters and local history to the newspapers.

---

155. GEORGE CRAWFORD[6] BEEKMAN, born July 2d, 1839, married November 6th, 1877, Laura B. Alston, born March 2d, 1852, daughter of Abraham D. Alston. He was graduated from Princeton University in the class of 1859, and received the degrees of A. B. and A. M. He was admitted to the New Jersey bar in 1863, and the same year began the practice of law at Freehold, remaining there until 1903, when he removed with his family to Red Bank, where he now resides. He served as Law Judge of the Monmouth County Court 1869-1872, and was State Senator from the county 1879-1882. He has done considerable writing for the press on historical and genealogical subjects. Issue:

161. ALSTON[7] BEEKMAN, born July 1st, 1878, married Matilda M. Craig, daughter of John W. Craig and Matilda Mount. He was admitted to the New Jersey bar in 1903, and is engaged in the practice of law at Red Bank.

162. ANNA CRAWFORD[7] BEEKMAN, born April 9th, 1880, died December 16th, 1902.

163. JACOB TENBROEK[7] BEEKMAN, born May 19th, 1883.

164. EDWIN LAURENS[7] BEEKMAN, born August 25th, 1889.

---

84. ADALINE[5] CRAWFORD, born February 16th, 1803, died August 27th, 1886, married December 16th, 1822, John Lloyd Hendrickson, born March 3d, 1801, died September 25th, 1845, son of John Hendrickson and Mary Lloyd, and grandson of Daniel Hendrickson and Eleanor Van-Mater; resided on Hendrickson homestead farm at Middletown. Issue:

191. ELEANOR[6] HENDRICKSON, born October 9th, 1823, died October 22d, 1837.

192. ANN[6] HENDRICKSON, born September 26th, 1825, died in infancy.

193. GEORGE CRAWFORD[6] HENDRICKSON, born March 8th, 1829, died October 12th, 1875.

194. MARY LOUISA[6] HENDRICKSON, born January 26th, 1838, and now resides on the homestead.

63. CATHERINE[4] CRAWFORD, married Nathaniel Leonard. Issue:

201*. POLLY[5] LEONARD, married Samuel C. Mott.

201. POLLY[5] LEONARD, married Samuel C. Mott. Issue:

211. LEONARD[6] MOTT.

212. SAMUEL C.[6] MOTT.

213. ANN MARIA[6] MOTT.

214. JERUSHA[6] MOTT.

215. CLEMENTINA[6] MOTT.

216. CATHERINE[6] MOTT.

64. ESTHER[4] CRAWFORD, married Thomas Burrows. Issue:

221*. EDWARD[5] BURROWS, married Catherine[5] Crawford [81].

222*. RICHARD CRAWFORD[5] BURROWS, married Mary Taylor.

223. DEBORAH[5] BURROWS, married Richard Walling.

224. CATHERINE[5] BURROWS, married William Tilton.

221. EDWARD[5] BURROWS, married August 22d, 1815, Catherine[5] Crawford [81]. Issue:

231. A daughter[6], married Jacob McClane.

222. RICHARD CRAWFORD[5] BURROWS, married Mary Taylor, daughter of Joseph Taylor, who carried on a large tannery in Middletown. Issue:

241. THOMAS[6] BURROWS.

242. JOSEPH T.[6] BURROWS, born July 7th, 1837, married Sarah Lemmon, and resides at Red Bank.

65. HANNAH[4] CRAWFORD, buried May 23d, 1845, married March 9th, 1797, Timothy White, died 1842, son of Samuel and Jemima White of Shrewsbury. Issue:

251*. CATHERINE C.[5] WHITE, born February 28th, 1798, married Jarrett Morford.

252. JEMIMA[5] WHITE, died when about 14 years old.

251. CATHERINE C.[5] WHITE, born February 28th, 1798, died January 14th, 1869, married April 2d, 1818, Jarrett Morford of Red Bank, born May 3d, 1781, died September 21st, 1865, son of Thomas Morford and Hannah Holmes. Issue:

261. HANNAH[6] MORFORD, married James McCausland, a prominent merchant of New York City. Issue: Laura, Agnes.

262. ELIZABETH[6] MORFORD, died unmarried.

263*. THOMAS F.[6] MORFORD, married Elizabeth Wilbur.

264*. SAMUEL WHITE[6] MORFORD, born 1835, married Mary R. Ovens.

265*. ANNA[6] MORFORD, married William H. Grant.

266. HENRY HOBART[6] MORFORD.

263. THOMAS F.[6] MORFORD, died April, 1888, married Elizabeth Wilbur of Brooklyn, N. Y. Issue:

271. JANE[7] MORFORD, died young, unmarried.

272. CATHERINE[7] MORFORD.

273. LAURA[7] MORFORD, married Frederick Wyckoff.

274. HARRY[7] MORFORD.

264. SAMUEL WHITE[6] MORFORD, born 1835, married Mary R. Ovens of Albany, N. Y. He resides at the old Morford homestead on the Shrewsbury river, Red Bank, and has served as mayor of the city. He conducts a large coal and wood business at Red Bank, and was for many years a director of the First National Bank. Issue:

281. ANNA G.[7] MORFORD, married Walter G. French.

282. JARRETT[7] MORFORD.

283. NELLY[7] MORFORD, died young, unmarried.

284. ALICE E.[7] MORFORD.

285. LIVINGSTON[7] MORFORD, died in infancy.

265. ANNA[6] MORFORD, died March 5th, 1868, married 1854 William H. Grant of Middletown township. Issue:

291. LAURA[7] GRANT, died young, unmarried.

292. T. HENRY[7] GRANT, a civil engineer, who lives on the farm in Middletown township where his father resided.

---

53. WILLIAM[3] CRAWFORD, married, license dated December 27th, 1756, Catherine Bowne, daughter of John Bowne, who was the eldest son of Obadiah Bowne. Issue:

301*. JOHN[4] CRAWFORD, married Caroline Fields.

302*. WILLIAM[4] CRAWFORD, married Rebecca Patterson.

303*. ESTHER[4] CRAWFORD, born February 3d, 1761, married Robert White.

---

301. JOHN[4] CRAWFORD, married Caroline Fields, daughter of Elnathan Fields. His will, dated November 15th, 1834, was proved January 2d, 1835 (Monmouth Co. Wills, C. 436). Issue:

311. ANDREW[5] CRAWFORD, died young, unmarried.

312. WILLIAM[5] CRAWFORD, married Elizabeth Fields; no issue.

313. JOHN[5] CRAWFORD, died young, unmarried.

314. ELNATHAN[5] CRAWFORD, died young, unmarried.

315*. JAMES G.[5] CRAWFORD, born December 29th, 1794, married Elizabeth Smith.

---

315. JAMES G.[5] CRAWFORD, born December 29th, 1794, married Elizabeth Smith, daughter of William Smith. He lived on the homestead farm at Crawford's Corner in the present township of Holmdel. Issue:

321*. CAROLINE[6] CRAWFORD, born 1819, married Holmes Conover.

322*. ANN[6] CRAWFORD, born 1821, married Joseph H. Holmes.

323. MARY[6] CRAWFORD, born 1823, died young, unmarried.

324. WILLIAM S.[6] CRAWFORD, born November 15th, 1826, married 1867 Emeline L. Stillwell, daughter of John S. Stillwell, and resides on the homestead where his father lived.

325*. JOHN J.[6] CRAWFORD, born February 22d, 1829, married Mary Frost.

326. ELIZABETH[6] CRAWFORD, born 1837, and resides at the homestead with her brother, William S. Crawford.

---

321. CAROLINE[6] CRAWFORD, born 1819, died August 28th, 1843, married March 3d, 1841, Holmes Conover, born January 10th, 1808, died May 22d, 1860, son of Cornelius R. Conover and Mary Stoutenbergh of Pleasant Valley. He was twice sheriff of Monmouth County. Issue:

331. CRAWFORD[7] CONOVER, died young, unmarried.

---

322. ANN[6] CRAWFORD, born 1821, died June 6th, 1892, married September 19th, 1848, Joseph H. Holmes, son of Sheriff Daniel Holmes; resided on the old Holmes farm in Pleasant Valley. Issue:

341. CAROLINE[7] HOLMES, married Asher H. Ely of Freehold.

342. JOHN S.[7] HOLMES, married Anna Lake, and resides on homestead farm.

343. DANIEL[7] HOLMES.

344. ELIZABETH[7] HOLMES, died young, unmarried.

---

325. JOHN J.[6] CRAWFORD, born February 22d, 1829, died 1888, married 1855 Mary Frost of Chapel Hill. He purchased the old "Barnes Smock" farm in Holmdel township and there made his home. Of the following children, two sons and four daughters are living:

351. JOHN[7] CRAWFORD.

352. JAMES G.[7] CRAWFORD.

353. WILLIAM[7] CRAWFORD.

354. SARAH[7] CRAWFORD.

355. CAROLINE[7] CRAWFORD.

356. MARY[7] CRAWFORD.

357. ESTHER[7] CRAWFORD.

358. THERESA[7] CRAWFORD.

359. EMMA[7] CRAWFORD.

---

302. WILLIAM[4] CRAWFORD, married Rebecca Patterson, daughter of Jehu

Patterson of Middletown township. Issue;

361*. JOHN BOWNE[5] CRAWFORD, born 1789, married Catherine[5] Crawford [72].

362. WILLIAM[5] CRAWFORD, died young, unmarried.

363*. WILLIAM H.[5] CRAWFORD, married Leah Conover.

364*. JAMES PATTERSON[5] CRAWFORD, married Margaretta Bowne.

365*. ANN BOWNE[5] CRAWFORD, born June 25th, 1788, married Hendrick Conover.

---

361. JOHN BOWNE[5] CRAWFORD, born 1789, died 1865, married his second cousin CATHERINE[5] CRAWFORD [72]. She inherited all the Crawford homestead at Nutswamp, and here they resided. His will, dated February 25th, 1857, was proved September 8th, 1865 (Monmouth Co. Wills, H. 321). Issue:

371*. GEORGE W.[6] CRAWFORD, born December 15th, 1825, married Sarah Frost.

372. REBECCA S.[6] CRAWFORD, born July 20th, 1828, died April 17th, 1876, married Robert Allen, Jr., a well-known lawyer of Red Bank, who at one time served as Prosecutor of the Pleas of Monmouth Co.

373. ELIZABETH S.[6] CRAWFORD, born April 16th, 1832, died October 2d, 1836.

374. WILLIAM[6] CRAWFORD, born August 8th, 1834, died October 27th, 1836.

375. CATHERINE E.[6] CRAWFORD, born April 5th, 1837, died at Jamesburg, N. J., married John D. Buckelew, sheriff of Middlesex Co. and U. S. consul to Stettin, Germany. Their later home was at Jamesburg, N. J.; no issue.

376. RICHARD[6] CRAWFORD, born December 1st, 1838, died March, 1906, married November 21st, 1866, Julia Robinson, daughter of William Robinson of Sing Sing, N. Y. No issue.

---

371. GEORGE W.[6] CRAWFORD, born December 15th, 1825, died October 19th, 1878, married Sarah Frost of Chapel Hill. At the time of his death he farmed 500 acres and represented Middletown township on the Board of Chosen Freeholders of Monmouth Co. Issue:

381. JOHN B.[7] CRAWFORD.

382. RICHARD[7] CRAWFORD, died young, unmarried.

383. JAMES F.[7] CRAWFORD, who now owns and farms the greater part of the old Crawford homestead at Nutswamp.

---

363. WILLIAM H.[5] CRAWFORD, married Leah Conover, daughter of Cornelius R. Conover and Mary Stoutenbergh. They occupied that part of the Bowne homestead at Crawford's Corner in Holmdel township on which the large dwelling house stood erected by John Bowne some time between 1725 and 1740, and which has since been destroyed by fire. Issue:

391. HOLMES C.[6] CRAWFORD, deceased, married Evelyn Peterson.

392. WILLIAM H.[6] CRAWFORD, deceased, married Phebe A. Duryea.

393. JOHN B.[6] CRAWFORD, deceased, married Henrietta Schenck.

394. ALBRO B.[6] CRAWFORD, deceased.

395. CHARLES V.[6] CRAWFORD.

396. MARY JANE L.[6] CRAWFORD, deceased.

397. JAMESANNA L.[6] CRAWFORD.

398. SARAH ELIZABETH[6] CRAWFORD, deceased, married D. T. Polhemus.

399. KATHARINE BIBB[6] CRAWFORD, deceased, married Horace A. Field.

---

364. JAMES PATTERSON[5] CRAWFORD, married Margaretta Bowne, born 1817 and still living (1907) at the age of ninety. Issue:

401. WILLIAM W. CRAWFORD, died young.

402*. JOHN B.[6] CRAWFORD, married Mary Foley.

403. JAMES HARTSHORNE[6] CRAWFORD.

404. RICHARD BOWNE[6] CRAWFORD, deceased.

405*. ELLEN BOWNE[6] CRAWFORD, married James Clark Smith.

406. REBEKAH PATTERSON[6] CRAWFORD.

407. ALTHEA BRINCKERHOFF^6 CRAWFORD, married Arthur Parcells Cox of California.

408. MARY BOWNE^6 CRAWFORD, died 1883.

409. SIDNEY G.^{6} CRAWFORD.

---

402. JOHN B.^{6} CRAWFORD, died at 65, married Mary Foley. Issue:

411. KATRINA^7 CRAWFORD.

412. MARGARETTA^7 CRAWFORD.

413. ELLEN^7 CRAWFORD.

414. ANNIE^7 CRAWFORD.

415. AGNES^7 CRAWFORD.

416. ROBERT LEE^7 CRAWFORD, deceased.

417. GROVER CLEVELAND^7 CRAWFORD, deceased.

---

405. ELLEN BOWNE^6 CRAWFORD, married James Clark Smith of Baltimore, deceased. Issue:

421. SAMUEL WYMAN^7 SMITH.

422. LINDA CLARK^7 SMITH.

---

365. ANN BOWNE^5 CRAWFORD, born June 25th, 1788, died February 10th, 1832, married Hendrick Conover, born 1773, died September 17th, 1835, son of Jacob Conover and Mary Schenck. Issue:

431. WILLIAM CRAWFORD^6 CONOVER, born June 23d, 1808, died August 8th, 1817.

432. JACOB^6 CONOVER, born 1810, died December 24th, 1846, married Ellen L. Vanderveer, born 1816, died September 24th, 1846; had three daughters.

433*. REBECCA^6 CONOVER, married Tunis J. Conover.

434. MARY^6 CONOVER, married Judge James S. Lawrence of Upper Freehold.

435. ANN^6 CONOVER, married Charles Belden.

436. CATHERINE^6 CONOVER, married Dr. William Johnson Conover, son of John I. Conover and Lydia Johnson.

---

433. REBECCA^6 CONOVER, married Tunis J. Conover. Issue:

441. HENDRICK^7 CONOVER, married ——— Taylor, daughter of George Taylor.

442. WILLIAM I.^{7} CONOVER, married Susan Smock.

---

303. ESTHER^4 CRAWFORD, born February 3d, 1761, died May 10th, 1797, married July 13th, 1780, Robert White, born November 24th, 1753, died 1831 or prior. Issue:

451. CRAWFORD^5 WHITE, born June 14th, 1782, married December 9th, 1819, Ann Taylor, daughter of Joel and Ann Taylor.

452*. CATHERINE^5 WHITE, born March 25th, 1784, married Isaac Martin, Jr.

453. TYLEE^5 WHITE, born October 29th, 1786, died September 28th, 1802.

454. ROBERT BOWNE^5 WHITE, born October 17th, 1788.

455. LYDIA GROVER^5 WHITE, born December 20th, 1791, married March 16th, 1814, Rev. Samuel P. Lewis, and had one daughter and two sons.

456*. WILLIAM C.^{5} WHITE, born September 8th, 1794, married Mary Barnes.

---

452. CATHERINE^5 WHITE, born March 25th, 1784, married June 11th, 1807, Isaac Martin, Jr. Issue:

461. BENJAMIN^6 MARTIN.

---

456. WILLIAM C.^{5} WHITE, born September 8th, 1794, died June 13th, 1880, married Mary Barnes, born March 10th, 1796, died February 6th, 1897. Issue:

471. JOSEPH^6 WHITE.

472. ROBERT^6 WHITE.

473. ELIZABETH^6 WHITE.

474. CRAWFORD^6 WHITE.

---

54. JOB^3 CRAWFORD, died 1770, married, license dated November 25th, 1766, Ann Morris, who survived him; resided at Middletown, N. J. His will, dated May 4th, 1770, was proved August 11th, 1770. (Trenton Wills, K. 234.) Issue:

481. JOSHUA^4 CRAWFORD.

482. GEORGE^4 CRAWFORD.

56. LYDIA[3] CRAWFORD, married 1st, license dated July 30th, 1756, Cornelius Compton of Middletown, by whom she is said to have had two sons; married 2d, 1767, Benjamin Morris. Issue:

491. ———[4] COMPTON.

492. ———[4] COMPTON.

493. BENJAMIN[4] MORRIS, born 1768, married and had six children, two of whom were named Charles and Benjamin.

494. JOSEPH[4] MORRIS, born 1770, married Patience (Herbert ?).

495. STOUT[4] MORRIS.

496. LYDIA[4] MORRIS, married James Frost.

497. ESTHER[4] MORRIS, married October 27th, 1799, Jonathan Stout.

THE CRAWFORD FAMILY.

John Crawford, the first of the family in this country, came from Ayrshire, Scotland, about 1672. He first settled in Massachusetts, then in Long Island, and came to Middletown, N. J., as early as 1678. He is first mentioned in the New Jersey records in a deed from Richard Gibbons and wife, dated December 11th, 1678, conveying to him a house lot in the village of Middletown assigned to the grantor in the first division of the land in 1667 under the Nichols Patent. The original deed was in the possession of the family for 227 years until 1905, when it was presented to the Monmouth Co. Historical Society. (Monmouth Co. Deeds, A. See fac-simile in Hist. and Biog. Atlas of N. J. Coast, p. 69.) Two tracts of land in Monmouth Co., one at "Waykake," were conveyed to John Crawford by patent from the Proprietors of East Jersey March 25th, 1687, and the homestead tract at Nutswamp was secured by another patent December 3d, 1687. (Trenton Deeds, B. 211, 510.) John Crawford was engaged in the whaling industry from his first settlement in Monmouth Co. He is named among the twelve men in the county to whom a charter was granted February 4th, 1679, to take whales off the Monmouth coast. It was this business no doubt which led him with his wife Elizabeth and son George to remove in 1693 to Cape May Co. Whales were then frequenting the waters of Delaware Bay, where it was easier to catch them than in the open sea. Between 1691 and 1694 a number of men from Monmouth Co. and Long Island founded a town called Portsmouth on the Delaware Bay side in the lower township of Cape May Co. about three miles north of the point. The earliest deed for real estate at Portsmouth was made April 1st, 1699, to John Crawford for 300 acres. He and his wife died here in 1705, her death occurring one month previous to his decease, and the inventory of his goods and chattels was presented by his son George December 11th of that year. He had at least two sons, John and George, and may have had two others, Richard and Joshua, for these names appear early in the records of Cape May Co.

John Crawford, Jr., remained in Monmouth Co. His father conveyed land to him by deed signed August 3d, 1691, but not acknowledged and delivered until March 9th, 1693. (Trenton Deeds, F. 739; Monmouth Deeds, A. 36.) He also received from his father the tract at Nutswamp, which has been the Crawford homestead for so many generations. John Crawford, Jr., was grand juror in 1693. He married 1698 or prior Abigail ————, and had at least one son, George Crawford, who married about 1726 Esther Scott [11], the daughter of John Scott [1] and Mary Bills.

THE SHEPHERD FAMILY.

Joseph Shepherd of Middletown, by occupation a miller, was the son of Thomas Shepherd, who died May 17th, 1751, aged about 73 years. He married May 19th, 1733, Rebecca Lippet, and died September 1st, or 2d, 1753. His will, dated September 1st, 1753, was proved September 10th, 1753. (Trenton Wills, F. 134.) Issue:

(1) Catherine, born August 11th, 1734, married Richard Crawford [52*].

(2) Deborah, born December 22d, 1735.

(3) Sarah, a twin, born September 1st, 1737, died unmarried January 4th, 1835, and is buried in the Murray family plot in the Baptist Church Burying Ground, Middletown.

(4) Mary, a twin, born September 1st, 1737.

(5) Hannah, born September 11th, 1739.

(6) Thomas, born June 22d, 1741.

(7) Moses, born October 25th, 1743.

THE BOWNE FAMILY.

William Bowne came with his wife Ann and oldest son John from Yorkshire, England, and settled at Salem, Mass., in 1631. He afterwards removed to Gravesend, L. I., and bought a plantation there November 12th, 1646. Early in 1665 he came to New Jersey and settled in Monmouth County. He married 2d, July 12th, 1669, Mary H. Felt, and died at Portland Point (Atlantic Highlands) in 1677. His children, all by his first wife, were as follows:

(1) Captain John Bowne (a), born in England, died January 3d, 1684, married Lydia Holmes, daughter of Rev. Obadiah and Catherine Holmes.

(2) James Bowne, baptized in Salem, Mass., August 25th, 1636, died 1692, married 1665 Mary Stout, daughter of Richard Stout and Penelope VanPrincis. Issue: Deborah, Sarah, Catherine, James, Andrew, John, William.

(3) Andrew Bowne, baptized in Salem, Mass., August 12th, 1638, died 1708, married Elizabeth ———. He was Deputy Governor of New Jersey in 1698. His daughter Elizabeth married her cousin Obadiah (b), son of Captain John Bowne.

(4) Philip Bowne, born 1640; resided at Flushing, L. I.

(a) Captain John Bowne and his wife Lydia Holmes had children as follows:

(1) Captain John Bowne, 2d, born April 1st, 1664, died March 13th, 1716, married, license dated December 26th, 1692, Frances Bowman; no issue.

(2) Obadiah Bowne (b), born July 18th, 1666, died April 19th, 1726, married 1st his cousin Elizabeth Bowne, daughter of Andrew Bowne; married 2d Elizabeth Longfield. His children, the first three by his first wife, were as follows: John (c), Ann, Lydia, Obadiah, Thomas, Cornelius, Mary.

(3) Deborah, or Dorothy, Bowne, born January 26th, 1668, married Gershom Mott.

(4) Sarah Bowne, born November 27th (or 23d), 1669, married Richard Salter. Issue: Hannah, John, Ebenezer, Richard, Thomas. The daughter Hannah married Mordecai Lincoln, who is believed to be an ancestor of President Abraham Lincoln.

(5) Catherine Bowne.

(c) John Bowne, son of Obadiah and Elizabeth Bowne, married Ann ———, and had children as follows:

(1) Catherine Bowne, married, license dated December 27th, 1756, William Crawford [53*].

(2) Lydia Bowne, married James Grover.

(3) Andrew Bowne.

(4) Ann Bowne.

IV.

Abraham White and Mehitable Scott.

13. MEHITABLE[2] SCOTT, born January 16th, 1707, married not later than 1735, ABRAHAM WHITE, of whose parentage nothing is known. They lived at Shrewsbury and are known to have had at least one son, but some or all of the following may have been their children: Amey White, married, license dated August 5th, 1765, William Tilton; Abigail White, married, license dated April 24th, 1766, Miln Parker; Robert White, married, license dated December 10th, 1768, Hannah Clark; Marcy White, married Uriah West. Issue:

501*. JOHN[3] WHITE, married 1st Catherine Olden and 2d Mary Smith.

---

501. JOHN[3] WHITE, married 1st Catherine Olden, daughter of James Olden of Stony Brook, and married 2d, license dated October 11th, 1782, Mary Smith, daughter of John and Hannah Smith. He early removed to Lawrenceville, near Trenton, N. J., and had six children, three by each wife, in the following order:

511. JOB[4] WHITE, died unmarried.

512. NANCY[4] WHITE, died unmarried.

513*. JAMES[4] WHITE, born 1778, married Martha Hendrickson.

514*. CATHERINE[4] WHITE, married Giles W. Olden.

515. BENJAMIN C.[4] WHITE, married Ann Paxson.

516. JONATHAN[4] WHITE, died unmarried.

---

513. JAMES[4] WHITE, born 1778, died 1851, married Martha Hendrickson, born 1771, died 1848, daughter of Philip Hendrickson and Charity Green. Issue:

521*. JOB[5] WHITE, married Mary C. Howell.

522*. ROBERT[5] WHITE, born 1800, married 1st Elizabeth Cook and 2d Mrs. Ruth Hunt Welling.

523*. WILLIAM[5] WHITE, married Hannah Haines.

524*. GEORGE[5] WHITE, married Mary C. Schenck.

525. JOHN[5] WHITE.

---

521. JOB[5] WHITE, married Mary C. Howell, daughter of Noah Howell and Hannah Lawrence. Issue:

531. ELIZABETH[6] WHITE, married Charles Henry Skirm.

532. MARTHA ANN[6] WHITE, died young.

533. JANE[6] WHITE, died young.

534*. BENJAMIN C.[6] WHITE, married Mary Rouse.

---

534. BENJAMIN C.[6] WHITE, married Mary Rouse, daughter of William Rouse. Issue:

541. ELIZABETH[7] WHITE, married Alonzo Howell.

542. MARTHA[7] WHITE.

---

522. ROBERT[5] WHITE, born 1800, died 1857, married 1st Elizabeth Cook, daughter of Daniel Cook, and married 2d Mrs. Ruth Hunt Welling, widow of Robert Welling. Issue by first wife:

551. SAMUEL[6] WHITE, died at 13 years of age.

---

523. WILLIAM[5] WHITE, married Hannah Haines. He was a merchant in

Philadelphia for many years, part of the time associated with Matthew Newkirk. Upon retirement from active business he removed to Trenton, where he lived until his death. Issue:

561. EPHRAIM[6] WHITE, died young.
562. GEORGE[6] WHITE.
563. ANNA[6] WHITE.
564. ELIZABETH[6] WHITE, died young.
565. JAMES[6] WHITE, died young.
566. MARIA ELIZABETH[6] WHITE.

---

524. GEORGE[5] WHITE, married Mary C. Schenck, daughter of Peter Z. Schenck of Pennington. He was a physician and lived in Lawrenceville. Issue:

571. LOUISA A.[6] WHITE.
572. JAMES E.[6] WHITE, died in childhood.
573. CATHERINE OLDEN[6] WHITE.
574. GEORGE SCHENCK[6] WHITE.
575. ROBERT[6] WHITE, a physician, settled at Riverton, Pa.; died young.

---

514. CATHERINE[4] WHITE, married Giles W. Olden, son of Samuel Olden and Mary Worth. Issue:

581. JOHN[5] OLDEN.
582. JAMES[5] OLDEN.
583. SAMUEL[5] OLDEN.

V.

William Scott and Mary Runnels.

15. WILLIAM^{2} SCOTT, born August 30th, 1712, died 1762, married November 27th, 1735, Mary Runnels. The wedding took place in the Friends' Meeting House at Shrewsbury, and among those present who signed as witnesses were his father John Scott, his brother Samuel Scott, his sisters Mehitable White and Hannah Scott, his cousin Mary Bills and a Jemima Runnels, some near relative of the bride. William Scott resided on the farm which had belonged to Abraham Vickars near Newman's Spring, and which, with other land, he inherited from his father's estate. The following description of the farm is found in a deed dated November 17th, 1736 (Monmouth County Deeds, H, 168), in which Samuel and John Scott sign a release giving the property to their brother William: "All that tract of land, situate, lying and being in Shrewsbury in the County of Monmouth afôresaid, which was given and bequeathed to our said brother William in and by the last will and testament of our father John Scott deceased, lying to the southward of our father's homestead farm and formerly belonging to Abraham Vickars, with all and every the buildings and appurtenances thereunto belonging, beginning at a chestnut tree marked near Newman's Spring on the bank of the river, and from thence eastwardly to within two rods of George Allen's Corner, and thence farther to a walnut sapling marked on three sides near the corner of a field, thence due east to Edmond Lefetra's land, together with the upper piece of meadow known by the name of Glassmakers' Landing." William Scott's will, dated November 30th, 1761, was proved August 20th, 1762. In it he directed that all his property should be sold and the proceeds divided among his eight children. (Trenton Wills, H, 176.) Issue:

601*. RICHARD^{3} SCOTT, married Mary Story.

602*. JOHN^{3} SCOTT, married Sarah Hisson.

603*. GEORGE^{3} SCOTT, married.

604*. JOB^{3} SCOTT, married.

605. RALPH WARNER^{3} SCOTT, living unmarried in Middlesex County in 1823; probably died unmarried.

606. SUSANNAH^{3} SCOTT.

607. HANNAH^{3} SCOTT.

608*. SARAH^{3} SCOTT, married David Tilton.

Note. It is probable that either Susannah or Hannah Scott married a Reid, though no record of it can be found, and had issue, James, William and Eleanor, for John Scott [611] son of Richard [601] mentions in his will "James Reed's daughter Sarah and any other sons or daughters which he may have living at the time of my decease, William Reid's daughter Margaret living at the Genesee Country, and Eleanor Reid my cousin."

---

601. RICHARD^{3} SCOTT, died 1815, married Mary Story, died 1822, daughter of John and Mary Story of South Brunswick. He owned and lived on a farm of [illegible]12 acres at Scott Corner, in the township of South Brunswick, about a mi[illegible]nd a half from Plainsboro, N. J. [illegible] farm

WILLIAM[4] SCOTT [621] AND HIS WIFE JANE THROCKMORTON.

was also the home of his son, who bequeathed it to his uncle John Scott [602] of Shrewsbury after the death of his mother, and at his death in 1831 it was sold in the settlement of the estate. Richard Scott's will, dated May 5th, 1810, was proved April 17th, 1815. The will of his wife Mary, dated March 26th, 1819, was proved January 26th, 1822. (Middlesex County Wills, B, 166, 535.) Issue:

611. JOHN[4] SCOTT, died 1817, married Mary Schenck, died 1841, daughter of John R. and Eve Schenck of Penn's Neck, West Windsor. He was a man of some wealth, and not only owned his father's homestead farm in the township of South Brunswick, where he lived, but also property in New Brunswick and at Penn's Neck. He bequeathed his estate to a number of uncles and cousins. His will, dated January 8th, 1817, was proved April 23d, 1817 (Middlesex County Wills, B, 280). The will of his wife, dated October 2d, 1839, was proved May 3d, 1841 (Somerset County Wills, E, 371).

---

602. JOHN[3] SCOTT, died October, 1831, married, license dated May 22d, 1779, Sarah Hisson, who survived him. He resided at Shrewsbury until he came into possession of his nephew's farm in South Brunswick, when this became his home until his death. His will, dated February 14th, 1824, was proved November 1st, 1831 (Middlesex Co. Wills, C, 448). Issue:

621*. WILLIAM[4] SCOTT, born April 16th, 1784, married Jane Throckmorton.

622*. JAMES[4] SCOTT, born about 1786, married Ann VanBrunt.

623. RALPH[4] SCOTT, married Isabella (Rue ?)

624. SARAH[4] SCOTT, married James Bennett, and is said to have had one son, who was a minister in the Methodist Episcopal Church.

625*. MARY[4] SCOTT, married Joseph Tilton.

626*. CATHERINE[4] SCOTT, married 1st Daniel Hulett and 2d Timothy White.

---

621. WILLIAM[4] SCOTT, born April 16th, 1784, died March 4th, 1874, married April 1st, 1810, Jane Throckmorton, born April 13th, 1791, at South River, N. J., died August 18th, 1885, daughter of Holmes Throckmorton and Susannah Forman. He was a tailor by trade, and was six feet or more in height. He resided first at Shrewsbury, and then at Eatontown, N. J., where both he and his wife died. They are both buried in the Quaker Burying Ground at Shrewsbury. Of his wife, Jane Throckmorton, Rev. T. S. Griffiths wrote in a letter which was read at her funeral, "She was the second person I baptized, March 16th, 1844, in the pond at Eatontown, and into the fellowship of the Red Bank Baptist Church." Issue:

631*. CATHERINE[5] SCOTT, born October 10th, 1810, married Captain Elisha Corlies Price.

632. SUSAN[5] SCOTT, born July 14th, 1813, died March 6th, 1832, married December 24th, 1831, James Lane.

633. JOHN[5] SCOTT, born September 24th, 1815, died March 18th, 1832.

634*. SARAH ANN[5] SCOTT, born October 8th, 1817, married Charles Tilton Fleming.

635*. HOLMES THROCKMORTON[5] SCOTT, born January 3d, 1820, married Eliza Field.

636*. JANE AMANDA[5] SCOTT, born May 6th, 1822, married Jacob Brower.

637*. MARY CAROLINE[5] SCOTT, born November 22d, 1826, married Walter Curtis Reynolds.

638*. WILLIAM WEBSTER[5] SCOTT, born November 6th, 1835, married Eleanor Dangler.

---

631. CATHERINE[5] SCOTT, born October 10th, 1810, at Shrewsbury, died June 27th, 1900, at Oceanport, N. J., married January 15th, 1835, Captain Elisha Corlies Price, born October 22d, 1805, died December 30th, 1853, son of Lawrence

Price and Catherine Taylor; resided at Oceanport, N. J. Issue:

641*. SUSAN ELIZABETH[6] PRICE, born December 8th, 1835, married William Hance Borden.

642*. JANE[6] PRICE, born March 21st, 1838, married Henry Brower.

643. JOHN CORLIES[6] PRICE, born October 2d, 1839; unmarried and resides at Virginia Beach, Va.

644. GEORGE SCOTT[6] PRICE, born July 26th, 1841, died January 13th, 1846.

645. THEODORE FREYLINGHUYSEN[6] PRICE, born September 15th, 1843, died August 11th, 1861.

646*. CAROLINE VIRGINIA[6] PRICE, born July 14th, 1845, married John Harris Cole.

647*. WINFIELD SCOTT[6] PRICE, born June 25th, 1847, married Annie Lufburrow Irwin.

648*. SARAH FLEMING[6] PRICE, born June 22d, 1849, married Jacob Edwin Corlies.

649. GEORGE[6] PRICE, born June 8th, 1852, died February 6th, 1853.

---

641. SUSAN ELIZABETH[6] PRICE, born December 8th, 1835, married October 22d, 1863, William Hance Borden, born September 5th, 1833, at Red Bank, N. J., son of Captain John Borden and Eliza Ann Lake; reside at Little Silver, N. J. Issue:

651. CARROLL[7] BORDEN, born November 10th, 1868, died November 21st, 1868.

---

642. JANE[6] PRICE, born March 21st, 1838, died April 5th, 1895, married November 19th, 1865, Henry Brower, born September 19th, 1831, at Long Branch, N. J., died April 25th, 1901, son of David Brower and Caroline Maps, and grandson of Cornelius Brower; resided at West Long Branch, N. J. Issue:

661*. CATHERINE PRICE[7] BROWER, born March 8th, 1868, married George Lincoln Gibbs.

662*. HENRY MAPS[7] BROWER, born December 18th, 1873, married Pearl Shack.

661. CATHERINE PRICE[7] BROWER, born March 8th, 1868, married January 21st, 1891, George Lincoln Gibbs, born March 26th, 1864, son of Samuel Louis Gibbs and Sarah Lane; reside at West Long Branch, N. J. Issue:

671. BASIL RUNGE[8] GIBBS, born September 14th, 1892, died February 20th, 1907.

672. MARION[8] GIBBS, born October 10th, 1898.

---

662. HENRY MAPS[7] BROWER, born December 18th, 1873, married June 28th, 1903, Pearl Shack, born January 19th, 1887, daughter of George Henry Shack and Susan Dangler; reside at West Long Branch, N. J. Issue:

681. VERA CAROLINE[8] BROWER, born October 21st, 1904.

---

646. CAROLINE VIRGINIA[6] PRICE, born July 14th, 1845, married February 28th, 1871, John Harris Cole, born March 20th, 1842, in New York City, son of Isaac P. Cole and Margaret Harris; resided in New York City, but now living near Red Bank, N. J. Issue:

691. ARTHUR STANLEY[7] COLE, born December 18th, 1871; studied at New York University and Crozer Theological Seminary, ordained to the Christian ministry February 26th, 1896, and now pastor of the First Baptist Church, Manasquan, N. J.

692*. JOHN PRICE[7] COLE, born November 27th, 1873, married Florence Woodhull Alling.

---

692. JOHN PRICE[7] COLE, born November 27th, 1873, married June 10th, 1896, Florence Woodhull Alling, born September 3d, 1874, daughter of William Tennent Alling and Emma Vanderveer Hendrickson; reside at Pittsburg, Pa. Issue:

711. ALLING[8] COLE, born April 1st, 1897.

---

647. WINFIELD SCOTT[6] PRICE, born June 25th, 1847, married November 19th, 1869, Annie Lufburrow Irwin, born

October 18th, 1847, at Middletown, N. J., daughter of William Conard Irwin and Eleanor Hyres Bennett; residence at Oceanport, N. J. Issue:

721. ELEANOR CATHERINE[7] PRICE, born March 12th, 1870.

722. ELISHA CORLIES[7] PRICE, born January 27th, 1874, died June 12th, 1904.

---

648. SARAH FLEMING[6] PRICE, born June 22d, 1849, married December 15th, 1880, Jacob Edwin Corlies, born January 10th, 1844, at Oceanport, N. J., son of Captain John Pintard Corlies and Emeline Woolley; reside in the Price homestead at Oceanport, N. J. Issue:

731. KATHRYN EMELYN[7] CORLIES, born April 1st, 1882, married May 4th, 1905, Joel Purcell Corin, born May 8th, 1883, son of Michael M. Corin and Sarah Robinson; reside in New York City.

---

634. SARAH ANN[5] SCOTT, born October 8th, 1817, died March 4th, 1896, married May 6th, 1838, Charles Tilton Fleming, born July 14th, 1815, died August 1st, 1894, son of Joseph Fleming and Lydia White, and grandson of Jacob Fleming; resided at Freehold, N. J. Issue:

741*. CAROLINE[6] FLEMING, born January 21st, 1839, married Charles Hendrickson Golden.

742*. AMANDA BROWER[6] FLEMING, born October 6th, 1840, married John Mount.

743. ARTHUR[6] FLEMING, born January 25th, 1842, died April 30th, 1854.

744*. CHARLES HENRY CLAY[6] FLEMING, born February 15th, 1844, married Mary Elizabeth Martin.

745. LOUISA[6] FLEMING, born December 23d, 1850, died August 18th, 1852.

746*. LOUISA[6] FLEMING, born December 18th, 1852, married John Livingston Conover.

747. KATE[6] FLEMING, born September 19th, 1856, died March 8th, 1857.

---

741. CAROLINE[6] FLEMING, born January 21st, 1839, died March 7th, 1884, married January 12th, 1859, Charles Hendrickson Golden, born February 19th, 1837, died November 14th, 1880, son of Cyrenus Golden and Ann Morris; resided at West Long Branch, N. J. Issue:

751. GEORGE[7] GOLDEN, born December 1st, 1859, died July 7th, 1875.

752*. ARTHUR FLEMING[7] GOLDEN, born April 19th, 1861, married Harriet Wolcott.

753. CATHERINE[7] GOLDEN, born January 25th, 1863, married Jesse B. Phillips.

754. CHARLES[7] GOLDEN, born April 26th, 1864, died August 17th, 1864.

755. WILLIAM[7] GOLDEN, born October 2d, 1865, died July 2d, 1866.

756. HARRY[7] GOLDEN, born February 16th, 1867, died April 21st, 1883.

757. LOUISE[7] GOLDEN, born May 23d, 1870, married Ephraim Meghan.

---

752. ARTHUR FLEMING[7] GOLDEN, born April 19th, 1861, married June 7th, 1883, Harriet Wolcott, born October 3d, 1861, daughter of Lewis Wolcott and Ann Kelsey; reside at West Long Branch, N. J. Issue:

761. IDA MAPS[8] GOLDEN, born July 23d, 1887.

762. JESSIE[8] GOLDEN, born April 19th, 1891.

---

742. AMANDA BROWER[6] FLEMING, born October 6th, 1840, married September 28th, 1859, John Mount, born March 28th, 1838, died June 21st, 1878, son of James Mount and Elizabeth Gardner; resided at West Long Branch, but now at Freehold, N. J. Issue:

771*. CHARLES FLEMING[7] MOUNT, born November 21st, 1861, married Margaı Hayden.

772. ELIZABETH[7] MOUNT, born September 12th, 1865, married July 23d, 1885, Herbert Weeks, born October 3d, 1862, son of William Weeks and Rachel Cooper; reside at Freehold, N. J.; no issue.

---

771. CHARLES FLEMING[7] MOUNT, born

November 21st, 1861, married Margaret Hayden, daughter of Samuel Hayden and Louisa West; reside at Long Branch, N. J. Issue:

781. JULIA ELIZABETH[8] MOUNT, born March 4th, 1894.

---

744. CHARLES HENRY CLAY[6] FLEMING, born February 15th, 1844, died August 27th, 1878, married March 17th, 1872, Mary Elizabeth Martin, daughter of John Martin. He served for three years during the Civil War as a non-commissioned officer in Co. I, 11th N. J. Volunteers, having previously served three months as a private. Issue:

791. GEORGIANA[7] FLEMING.

792. LILLIAN[7] FLEMING, married James Tindall, has one son, and resides at Windsor, N. J.

---

746. LOUISA[6] FLEMING, born December 18th, 1852, married John Livingston Conover, born February 21st, 1849, son of Alfred Livingston Conover and Eleanor Schenck Conover; reside at Wickatunk, N. J. Issue:

811. CHARLOTTE LYELL[7] CONOVER.

812. JOHN LIVINGSTON[7] CONOVER, JR.

813. EDWARD WOLPHERTSEN[7] CONOVER.

814. CHARLES FLEMING[7] CONOVER.

815. SARA ALIDA[7] CONOVER.

816. ALFRED LIVINGSTON[7] CONOVER.

817. DAISY LOUISA[7] CONOVER.

818. VIRGINIA STEELE[7] CONOVER.

819. STACEY PRICKET[7] CONOVER.

820. HAROLD VANDUYN[7] CONOVER.

---

635. HOLMES THROCKMORTON[5] SCOTT, born January 3d, 1820, deceased, married November 15th, 1847, Eliza Field, born June 7th, 1828, daughter of Benjamin Field and Rebecca Newlin. He served nine months in Co. D, 29th N. J. Volunteers, during the Civil War; resided at Matawan, N. J. Issue:

821. CHARLES AUGUSTUS[6] SCOTT, born December, 1849, married May 11th, 1875, Ella M. Swan, born October 15th, 1851, died June 4th, 1904, daughter of John B. Swan and Ann Maria Jones. He was for many years Chief of the Fire Department at Matawan, N. J.

822*. REBECCA[6] SCOTT, born August 28th, 1852, married 1st William Smith and 2d Arthur Bennett.

823*. ELIZABETH[6] SCOTT, married Harrison Denise.

824*. WALTER[6] SCOTT, married Emma Bogert.

825. WILLIAM[6] SCOTT, died when four years old.

826. EMMA[6] SCOTT, died when nine years old.

827*. GEORGIANA[6] SCOTT, married Frederick Greben.

828*. WILLIAM[6] SCOTT, married Elvira Walling.

---

822. REBECCA[6] SCOTT, born August 28th, 1852, deceased, married 1st William Smith, deceased, and 2d Arthur Bennett, born in England, deceased. Issue:

831. CHARLES[7] SMITH, died young.

832. ARTHUR[7] SMITH, died young.

833. IDA MAY[7] SMITH, died young.

834. WILFRID EUSTACE[7] BENNETT, living with his father's family in England.

---

823. ELIZABETH[6] SCOTT, deceased, married Harrison Denise, as his second wife. Issue:

841. WALTER[7] DENISE.

---

824. WALTER[6] SCOTT, deceased, married Emma Bogert. Issue:

851. CHARLES[7] SCOTT, died young.

---

827. GEORGIANA[6] SCOTT, deceased, married Frederick Greben, deceased. Issue:

861. LILA ELIZA[7] GREBEN, born August 8th, 1889.

---

828. WILLIAM[6] SCOTT, married Elvira Walling; reside at Matawan, N. J. Issue:

871. CAROLINE[7] SCOTT, died young.

---

636. JANE AMANDA[5] SCOTT, born May 6th, 1822, died January 4th, 1892, married February 15th, 1841, Jacob Brower, born

December 6th, 1817, at Locust Point, N. J., died March 6th, 1854, son of John A. Brower and Elizabeth Burdge; resided at Brooklyn, N. Y. Issue:

881*. MARY ELIZABETH[6] BROWER, born February 18th, 1842, married Charles Wesley Phillips.

882*. CAROLINE VIRGINIA[6] BROWER, born June 2d, 1844, married Eduardo Antonio Steele.

883*. HOLMES THROCKMORTON[6] BROWER, born October 12th, 1846, married Mary Elizabeth Fallon.

884*. SARAH JANE[6] BROWER, born February 22d, 1848, married Charles E. Hendrickson.

885*. WILLIAM SCOTT[6] BROWER, born May 20th, 1852, married 1st Margery Plant, and 2d Anna Bausch.

886*. MARIA ALTHEA[6] BROWER, born September 20th, 1854, married Thomas Oliver Duncan.

---

881. MARY ELIZABETH[6] BROWER, born February 18th, 1842, married June 28th, 1863, Charles Wesley Phillips, born December 27th, 1837, died October 24th, 1866, son of John Taylor Phillips and Harriet Edwards; resides at Brooklyn, N. Y. Issue:

891*. ELLA F.[7] PHILLIPS, born May 7th, 1865, married George E. Collins.

---

891. ELLA F[7]. PHILLIPS, born May 7th, 1865, married June 25th, 1886, George E. Collins, born March 31st, 1864, son of William Collins and Hannah E. Fenn; reside at Westfield, N. J. Issue:

901. CHARLES WESLEY[8] COLLINS, born October 15th, 1887.

902. MARY EVELIE[8] COLLINS, born December 29th, 1889.

---

882. CAROLINE VIRGINIA[6] BROWER, born June 2d, 1844, died September 1st, 1897, married Eduardo Antonio Steele, born August 6th, 1845, at Barranquilla, U. S. of Colombia, S. A., died April 21st, 1894; resided at Barranquilla, U. S. of Colombia, and Brooklyn, N. Y. The following children, with one exception, were born at Barranquilla:

911. EDWARD[7] STEELE, born August 13th, 1867, died June 21st, 1871.

912. AMANDA[7] STEELE, born April 15th, 1870, died 1872.

913*. MARY[7] STEELE, born April 28th, 1872, married Anibal Perez L.

914. IDA MAY[7] STEELE, born January 26th, 1877, at Brooklyn, N. Y., married June 15th, 1907, William Edward Brown; reside at Brooklyn, N. Y.

915. JOHN ARTHUR[7] STEELE, born January 3d, 1884; resides at Brooklyn, N. Y.

---

913. MARY[7] STEELE, born April 28th, 1872, married Anibal Perez L. as his second wife. He was born June 26th, 1855, at Carthagena, U. S. of Colombia, and resides at Barranquilla, U. S. of C. [NOTE: In the name Perez L., Perez is the family name of his father, and L. stands for Lopez, the family name of his mother. In Spanish countries it is often customary to combine the two and write them either Perez L. or Perez et Lopez. His children would not thus use his mother's name, but that of their own mother.] Issue, all born at Barranquilla:

921. NESTOR[8] PEREZ, born July 31st, 1890.

922. ESTEVAN[8] PEREZ, born November 29th, 1891.

923. EDUARDO[8] PEREZ, born April 27th, 1893.

924. VIRGINIA[8] PEREZ, born June 29th, 1894.

925. RICARDO[8] PEREZ, born January 26th, 1896.

926. MARY[8] PEREZ, born July 9th, 1897.

927. ANIBAL[8] PEREZ, born April 7th, 1899.

928. IDA[8] PEREZ, born February 1st, 1901, died November 26th, 1902.

---

883. HOLMES THROCKMORTON[6] BROWER, born October 12th, 1846, married Mary Elizabeth Fallon; resides at Brooklyn, N. Y. Issue:

931*. KATHERINE V.[7] BROWER, born December 27th, 1868, married Bradley Rockefeller.

932. HOLMES[7] BROWER, born May 17th, 1870.

933. EDWARD[7] BROWER, born December 7th, 1876, died August, 1903.

934. ELIZABETH[7] BROWER, born December 23d, 1881.

935. MARY[7] BROWER, born August 2d, 1885.

936. FREDERICK[7] BROWER, born 1887.

937. ANNIE[7] BROWER, born 1889.

938. ALICE[7] BROWER, born 1891.

939. AGNES[7] BROWER, born January 2d, 1893, died February 6th, 1893.

---

931. KATHERINE V.[7] BROWER, born December 27th, 1868, married Bradley Rockefeller; reside at Brooklyn, N. Y. Issue:

941. MARY E.[8] ROCKEFELLER, born September 4th, 1891.

942. LILLIAN[8] ROCKEFELLER, born December 29th, 1892.

943. AGNES[8] ROCKEFELLER, born August 19th, 1894, died July 5th, 1895.

944. BRADLEY[8] ROCKEFELLER, born December 1st, 1898.

945. GLADYS[8] ROCKEFELLER, born September 3d, 1903.

---

884. SARAH JANE[6] BROWER, born February 22d, 1848, died April, 1886, married Charles E. Hendrickson, born August 22d, 1849, son of Edward and Mary Hendrickson of Tinton Falls, N. J.; resided at Brooklyn, N. Y. Issue:

951. WILLIAM B.[7] HENDRICKSON, born November 3d, 1874, died May, 1875.

952. GEORGE L.[7] HENDRICKSON, born August 11th, 1876, died February, 1883.

953*. LILLIAN[7] HENDRICKSON, born March 28th, 1878, married Ralph A. Maul.

954. IDA B.[7] HENDRICKSON, born February 5th, 1881, married Marsden Coates; reside at Brooklyn, N. Y.

---

953. LILLIAN[7] HENDRICKSON, born March 28th, 1878, married Ralph A. Maul, son of Rev. W. R. Maul; reside at Suffern, N. Y. Issue:

961. EDWARD[8] MAUL, born 1898.

962. RUTH[8] MAUL, born November, 1902.

---

885. WILLIAM SCOTT[6] BROWER, born May 20th, 1852, died November 23d, 1897, married 1st Margery Plant, died December, 1886; married 2d Anna Bausch, who survives him; resided at Brooklyn, N. Y., and Union Hill, N. J. Issue, one by each marriage:

971. HAZEL[7] BROWER, born November, 1886, died December, 1887.

972. RENNIE[7] BROWER, born 1890.

---

886. MARIA ALTHEA[6] BROWER, born September 20th, 1854, married Thomas Oliver Duncan, born December 11th, 1859, son of Oliver Duncan and Jane Hughes; reside at Brooklyn, N. Y. Issue:

981. RICHARD OLIVER[7] DUNCAN, born October 26th, 1887.

---

637. MARY CAROLINE[5] SCOTT, born November 22d, 1826, married January 8th, 1845, Walter Curtis Reynolds, born January 8th, 1823, at Manasquan, N. J., died May 8th, 1893, son of John Miller Reynolds and Sarah Curtis; resides at Eatontown, N. J. Issue:

991*. CORLIES PRICE[6] REYNOLDS, born December 16th, 1845, married Sarah Jane Bennett.

992*. EBENEZER CURTIS[6] REYNOLDS, born August 2d, 1848, married Sarah Lavinia Howland.

993. SARAH JANE[6] REYNOLDS, born April 19th, 1852, married October 19th, 1875, George Allen Hope, born February 22d, 1851, son of Washington Lafayette Hope and Helen Cobb Allen; reside at Shrewsbury, N. J.; no issue.

994. JOHN MILLER[6] REYNOLDS, born June 24th, 1865, died September 30th, 1866.

---

991. CORLIES PRICE[6] REYNOLDS, born December 16th, 1845, married June 24th,

1865, Sarah Jane Bennett, born September 15th, 1845, daughter of James Bennett and Eliza Dangler; reside at Manasquan, N. J. Issue:

1001*. EVALINA MAY[7] REYNOLDS, born February 5th, 1867, married Charles Forman Gifford.

1001. EVALINA MAY[7] REYNOLDS, born February 5th, 1867, married January 13th, 1884, Charles Forman Gifford, born February 7th, 1861, son of John Brewer Gifford and Caroline Forman; reside at Allenwood, N. J. Issue:

1011. JOHN BREWER[8] GIFFORD, born August 25th, 1888.

1012. CORLIES PRICE[8] GIFFORD, born March 21st, 1891.

1013. HAROLD[8] GIFFORD, born March 1st, 1894.

1014. RAYMOND[8] GIFFORD, born February 20th, 1895.

1015. JENNIE N.[8] GIFFORD, born June 3d, 1897.

1016. SARAH C.[8] GIFFORD, born November 6th, 1899.

1017. LAURA F.[8] GIFFORD, born June 15th, 1903.

1018. ARCHIBALD HIGGINS[8] GIFFORD, born January 7th, 1906.

---

992. EBENEZER CURTIS[6] REYNOLDS, born August 2d, 1848, died October 31st, 1870, married June 19th, 1869, Sarah Lavinia Howland, born April 24th, 1849, daughter of Henry Wolcott Howland and Sarah Cook; resided at Eatontown, N. J. Issue:

1021*. WALTER EBENEZER[7] REYNOLDS, born November 8th, 1870, married Charlotte Watson Mershon.

1021. WALTER EBENEZER[7] REYNOLDS, born November 8th, 1870, married September 27th, 1900, Charlotte Watson Mershon, born April 16th, 1874, daughter of William Mershon and Julia Charlotte Watson. He studied at Peddie Institute and Crozer Theological Seminary, was ordained to the Christian ministry September 16th, 1897, at Raton, New Mexico, and is now pastor of the First Baptist Church, Woodbury, N. J. Issue:

1031. CHARLOTTE MERSHON[8] REYNOLDS, born August 22d, 1901.

1032. BERNICE MERSHON[8] REYNOLDS, born August 15th, 1902.

1033. VIRGINIA[8] REYNOLDS, born March 29th, 1907.

---

638. WILLIAM WEBSTER[5] SCOTT, born November 6th, 1835, died January 14th, 1893, married February 19th, 1864, Eleanor Dangler, born February 16th, 1845, daughter of Joseph Layton Dangler and Charlotte Howland; resided at Eatontown, N. J. Issue:

1041. STELLA MAY[6] SCOTT, born May 6th, 1865, died September 7th, 1866.

1042. THEODORE PRICE[6] SCOTT, born May 16th, 1867, died May 31st, 1893.

1043. JOSEPH DANGLER[6] SCOTT, born March 10th, 1869, died July 20th, 1869.

1044. SUSAN BORDEN[6] SCOTT, born June 24th, 1871, married July 3d, 1906, William Leon Walsh, born January 20th, 1873, son of John and Catherine Walsh; reside at Red Bank, N. J.

1045*. CHARLOTTE DANGLER[6] SCOTT, born August 12th, 1873, married Charles Augustus Newbury.

1046. JOHN PRICE[6] SCOTT, born October 24th, 1875; resides at Long Branch, N. J.

1047. GRACE[6] SCOTT, born August 19th, 1879, died September 6th, 1879.

1048. FRANK DANGLER[6] SCOTT, born February 29th, 1884, died March 1st, 1884.

1045. CHARLOTTE DANGLER[6] SCOTT, born August 12th, 1873, married February 1st, 1900, Charles Augustus Newbury, born October 25th, 1869, son of William Newbury and Louisa Newbury, his parents being cousins; reside at Long Branch, N. J. Issue:

1051. CHARLES EARLE[7] NEWBURY, born March 29th, 1901.

---

622. JAMES[4] SCOTT, born about 1786,

died June, 1813, married March 12th, 1813, Ann VanBrunt, died prior to 1868, daughter of Joseph C. VanBrunt and Mary Applegate; resided at Colt's Neck, N. J. His widow married 2d, February 1st, 1829, William I. Matthews of Shrewsbury. Issue:

1061*. JAMES[5] SCOTT, born December 13th, 1813, married Mary Ann Doughty.

1061. JAMES[5] SCOTT, born December 13th, 1813, died March 4th, 1886, married March 6th, 1842, Mary Ann Doughty, born April 3d, 1820, died April 10th, 1899, daughter of John Doughty and Elizabeth Llewellyn; resided at Fair Haven, N. J. Issue:

1071*. JOHN ROBERT[6] SCOTT, born August 24th, 1843, married Sarah Louisa Smith.

1072. JAMES[6] SCOTT, born September 21st, 1846, died December 3d, 1867.

1073*. WILLIAM CHAMPLAIN[6] SCOTT, born November 13th, 1850, married Lydia Ann Snedeker.

1074. SUSAN DOUGHTY[6] SCOTT, born June 14th, 1853, married January 12th, 1881, Edward Schoek VanLeer Stultz, born June 12th, 1854, son of Rev. Elias D. Stultz and Ellen S. Day; reside at Manasquan, N. J.; no issue.

1075*. DEWITT[6] SCOTT, born September 19th, 1855, married Ella Jeffrey.

1076*. ANNA[6] SCOTT, born July 11th, 1862, married Howard Corkey.

1071. JOHN ROBERT[6] SCOTT, born August 24th, 1843, married December 26th, 1865, Sarah Louisa Smith, born September 25th, 1844, daughter of Forman Smith and Sarah Rodgers; reside at Fair Haven, N. J. Issue:

1081*. FRANK[7] SCOTT, born December 15th, 1868, married Caroline Elizabeth Tattam.

1082. LESTER J.[7] SCOTT, born June 2d, 1873, died June 22d, 1879.

1081. FRANK[7] SCOTT, born December 15th, 1868, married December 21st, 1891, Caroline Elizabeth Tattam, born January 15th, 1871, daughter of George James Tattam and Elizabeth Ann Tetly, both of whom were born in England in 1843; reside at Newark, N. J. Issue:

1091. FLORENCE LOUISE[8] SCOTT, born July 9th, 1895.

1092. WALTER FRANKLYN[8] SCOTT, born June 23d, 1902.

1073. WILLIAM CHAMPLAIN[6] SCOTT, born November 13th, 1850, died June 23d, 1906, married January 18th, 1874, Lydia Ann Snedeker, born February 23d, 1852, died December 16th, 1895, daughter of Lambert L. Snedeker and Phebe F. Mitchell; resided at Fair Haven, N. J. Issue:

1101*. MAUD[7] SCOTT, born May 17th, 1875, married Herbert E. Snyder.

1102. JEANNETTE[7] SCOTT, born September 21st, 1885.

1101. MAUD[7] SCOTT, born May 17th, 1875, married September 14th, 1895, Herbert E. Snyder, born July 14th, 1876, son of George B. Snyder and Phebe Patterson; reside at Fair Haven, N. J. Issue:

1111. MYRTLE[8] SNYDER, born March 19th, 1900.

1112. HERBERT VERNON[8] SNYDER, born August 6th, 1902.

1075. DEWITT[6] SCOTT, born September 19th, 1855, married Ella Jeffrey, daughter of John Jeffrey and Delia Springsteen. Issue:

1121. HELENA[7] SCOTT.

1122. JAMES EDWARD[7] SCOTT.

1076. ANNA[6] SCOTT, born July 11th, 1862, married December 31st, 1884, Howard Corkey, born February 1st, 1854, son of Odell Corkey and Elizabeth Aldrich; resides at Manasquan, N. J. Issue:

1131. BESSIE LLEWELLYN[7] CORKEY, born March 22d, 1886.

1132. MARJORIE[7] CORKEY, born June 30th, 1889.

1133. IRENE[7] CORKEY, born January 27th, 1892.

625. MARY[4] SCOTT, died prior to 1824, married December 23d, 1804, Joseph Tilton. Issue:

1161. JOHN[5] TILTON, married and has descendants.

626. CATHERINE[4] SCOTT, born about 1790, died 1873, married 1st December 13th, 1816, Daniel Hulett, died March 8th, 1838, son of Thomas Hulett; married 2d May 13th, 1846, Timothy White, born March 28th, 1789, died September 6th, 1860, son of Joseph White and Mary Hart. Her will, dated July 18th, 1870, was proved March 22d, 1873 (Monmouth Co. Wills, L, 66). She resided at or near Red Bank, N. J., and had children only by her first husband as follows:

1181*. MARY[5] HULETT, born February 14th, 1821, married Jacob Longstreet.

1182*. MICHAEL[5] HULETT, born June 18th, 1823, married 1st Mary Ann Morris and 2d Mary Jane Woods.

1183*. HANNAH[5] HULETT, born July 8th, 1825, married John Vanderbilt.

1184. MARGARET[5] HULETT, born (April?) 18th, 1827, married 1st, February 9th, 1845, John Riddle Longstreet, a brother of Jacob Longstreet who married her sister, and married 2d Mr. Thomas; removed to Indiana.

1185. SUSAN LANE[5] HULETT, born September 1st, 1832, died January 9th, 1839.

1181. MARY[5] HULETT, born February 14th, 1821, died June 14th, 1890, married March 10th, 1842, Jacob Longstreet, born April 7th, 1818, died January 31st, 1906, son of William and Christina Longstreet. Had nine children, the four not mentioned below dying very young.

1191*. EMILY[6] LONGSTREET, born July 12th, 1843, married Andrew Morrison.

1192*. ALONZO[6] LONGSTREET, born September 11th, 1845, married Jane Kittison.

1193. CATHERINE[6] LONGSTREET, died young, August 31st, 1851.

1194*. WALTER[6] LONGSTREET, born October 10th, 1850, married Lydia Sherman.

1195. T. SCOTT[6] LONGSTREET, born August 25th, 1852, died December 19th, 1873.

1191. EMILY[6] LONGSTREET, born July 12th, 1843, died June 5th, 1903, married August 4th, 1864, Andrew Morrison, born March 19th, 1839, in Scotland, died May 5th, 1891. Issue:

1201. JOSEPHINE[7] MORRISON, born May 4th, 1866, died February 4th, 1867.

1202. LILLIAN[7] MORRISON, born June 4th, 1868, died January 15th, 1876.

1203*. JESSIE BROCKETT[7] MORRISON, born August 16th, 1870, married Frank F. Supp.

1203. JESSIE BROCKETT[7] MORRISON, born August 16th, 1870, married April 15th, 1888, Frank F. Supp, born May 15th, 1860; reside at Red Bank, N. J. Issue:

1211. RUTH J.[8] SUPP, born March 9th, 1894, died July 29th, 1894.

1192. ALONZO[6] LONGSTREET, born September 11th, 1845, married Jane Kittison. Issue:

1221. EMMA[7] LONGSTREET, married 1st George Storms and 2d Samuel O. Depew.

1222. WALTER S.[7] LONGSTREET, born January 31st, 1885.

1194. WALTER[6] LONGSTREET, born October 10th, 1850, died July 14th, 1874, married Lydia Sherman. Issue:

1231. EUGENE[7] LONGSTREET, married.

1182. MICHAEL[5] HULETT, born June 18th, 1823, married 1st April 26th, 1849, Mary Ann Morris, daughter of Benjamin Morris and Margaret Chadwick; married 2d Mary Jane Woods, born 1837, died August 6th, 1881, daughter of William Woods and Eliza P. Lewis; resides at Red Bank, N. J. He had one child by the first marriage and four by the second as follows:

1241. EMMA A[6]. HULETT, born January 17th, 1851, married 2d Mr. Raymond; no issue.

1242*. DEBORAH ANN[6] HULETT, born March 6th, 1858, married Lawrence E. Rogers.

1243. GEORGE W.[6] HULETT, born February 4th, 1860, died January 28th, 1862.

1244. MARY MATILDA[6] HULETT, born November 30th, 1861.

1245. SARAH SICKLES[6] HULETT, born March 1st, 1868.

1242. DEBORAH ANN[6] HULETT, born March 6th, 1858, married March 5th, 1879, Lawrence E. Rogers, son of Ezekiel J. Rogers. Issue:

1251. CHARLES H.[7] ROGERS, married March, 1907, Anna Havens.

1252. CLAUDIUS A.[7] ROGERS.

1253. PAULINE E.[7] ROGERS.

1183. HANNAH[5] HULETT, born July 8th, 1825, died March 9th, 1878, married John Vanderbilt. Issue:

1261. SAMUEL[6] VANDERBILT.

1262. MELISSA[6] VANDERBILT, died when 21 years old, married Samuel Hoyt, son of Captain William S. Hoyt, who died before his wife.

1263. CATHERINE E.[6] VANDERBILT, born September 17th, 1853, died June 12th, 1854.

1264. LOTTIE F.[6] VANDERBILT, born November 11th, 1857, died March 31st, 1863.

1265. CHARLES[6] VANDERBILT, born July 19th, 1860, died September 25th, 1861.

1266. EDGAR[6] VANDERBILT, born July 22d, 1865, died September 6th, 1867.

---

603. GEORGE[3] SCOTT, who is probably the George Scott of Kingwood, Hunterdon County, on whose estate administration was granted May 14th, 1821, to Elizabeth Scott, presumably his widow. Issue:

1271. JOHN W.[4] SCOTT, who is described in the will of his cousin John Scott [611] as living near Quaker Town, presumably in Hunterdon County, and who was bequeathed property at Penn's Neck, Windsor township. He was one of the executors who probated the will in 1817.

---

604. JOB[3] SCOTT, who married twice, but the names of his wives are unknown. The first two children given below had different mothers. He is known to have had another daughter. It is not known certainly whether Ann Atchley was his daughter or his niece, but the fact that her husband Daniel Atchley leaves property in his will to the children of Job Scott [1281], son of Job [604], makes it probably correct to identify her with the unnamed daughter which tradition gives to Job Scott. Issue:

1281*. JOB[4] SCOTT, married.

1282. SARAH[4] SCOTT, married ——— Woodward. She was living as late as 1834.

1283. ANN[4] SCOTT, married Daniel Atchley, died 1839. His will, dated September 8th, 1834, was proved May 3d, 1839. (Middlesex County Wills, D, 311.)

1281. JOB[4] SCOTT, married ———; resided in Philadelphia. Issue:

1291. BENJAMIN[5] SCOTT.

1292. RACHEL[5] SCOTT.

1293. SARAH[5] SCOTT.

---

608. SARAH[3] SCOTT, died February 9th, 1842, married David Tilton, born July 20th, 1749, died 1840, son of Robert Tilton and Miriam Allen. Issue:

1331*. WILLIAM[4] TILTON, born July (or August) 4th, 1773, married Margaret Corlies.

1332*. DAVID[4] TILTON, born January 8th, 1785, married probably Sarah Flemnen.

1331. WILLIAM[4] TILTON, born July (or August) 4th, 1773, died May, 1841, married March 8th, 1795, Margaret Corlies, born November 17th, 1775, daughter of Timothy Corlies and Lydia Allen. His will, dated May 19th, 1841, was proved June 4th, 1841. (Monmouth County Wills, D, 337.) Issue:

1341. SARAH[5] TILTON, born April 5th, 1797.

1342. LYDIA CORLIES[5] TILTON, born April 16th, 1799, married February 14th, 1837, Samuel Holmes.

1343*. CORLIES[5] TILTON, born August 26th, 1802, married Deborah H. White.

1344. ESECK[5] TILTON, born December 24th, 1805.

1345*. WILLIAM[5] TILTON, born April 7th, 1813, married Elizabeth Honce.

1343. CORLIES[5] TILTON, born August 26th, 1802, died August 13th, 1869, married January 24th, 1832, Deborah H. White, born June 2d, 1807, died March 13th, 1884, daughter of Amos White and Ann Throckmorton. Issue:

1351. MARGARET ANN[6] TILTON, born November 16th, 1832, married 1st Thomas Blanche and 2d Oliver Holmes.

1352. CHARLES H.[6] TILTON, born February 4th, 1835, married Kate Drum.

1353*. WILLIAM AMOS[6] TILTON, born May 14th, 1837, married Caroline Maghan.

1354. SARAH S.[6] TILTON, born December 10th, 1838, married December 13th, 1864, William L. Cromwell; resides on Long Island.

1355. JAMES WHITE[6] TILTON, born January 31st, 1841, married Kate ———, born 1842; resides at Marlboro, N. J.

1356*. LYDIA[6] TILTON, born September 9th, 1843, married Joseph White.

1353. WILLIAM AMOS[6] TILTON, born May 14th, 1837, died February 19th, 1908, married February 13th, 1866, Caroline Maghan, born April 13th, 1845, died June 25th, 1898; resided in Scobeyville, N. J. Issue:

1361. WILLIAM N.[7] TILTON.

1356. LYDIA[6] TILTON, born September 9th, 1843, died December 21st, 1899, married September 9th, 1875, Joseph White, son of James White and Mary Matthews. Issue:

1371. JAMES HOWARD[7] WHITE, born December 6th, 1876, married September 26th, 1900, Fannie Roberts, born July 26th, 1876.

1372. GEORGE EDMUND[7] WHITE, born May 20th, 1879, married December 18th, 1901, Lillian Bennett.

1345. WILLIAM[5] TILTON, born April 7th, 1813, died April 10th, 1887, married December 15th, 1837, Elizabeth Honce, born 1815, died February 23d, 1860, daughter of David Honce and Phebe VanKerk. Issue:

1381. MARGARET[6] TILTON, born 1838, married 1867 John J. Elkin; reside in New Brunswick, N. J.

1382. DAVID[6] TILTON, born June 20th, 1839, died 1856.

1383. ELIZABETH[6] TILTON, born August 14th, 1853, married February 25th, 1873, Albert Dennis, born July 19th, 1850; reside at Eatontown, N. J.

1384. HOLMES[6] TILTON, married Jennie VanDorn.

1332. DAVID[4] TILTON, born January 8th, 1785, died prior to March 16th, 1840, married probably, October 23d, 1806, Sarah Flemnen. Issue:

1391. ELIZABETH[5] TILTON, married January 5th, 1831, David K. Perrine.

1392. DAVID[5] TILTON, born June 29th, 1813, died March 3d, 1837, married Jane S. ———; she married 2d April 7th, 1839, James Brown.

THE THROCKMORTON FAMILY.

John Throckmorton (sometimes spelled Throgmorton), the ancestor of the Throckmortons of Monmouth County, N. J., came to this country in the ship *Lyon*, Captain Pierce master, embarking from Bristol, England, December 1st, 1630, and landing at Nantasket, near Boston, February 5th, 1631, after a very stormy voyage of sixty-five days. In the same ship came Roger Williams and his wife. No one knows certainly the English ancestry of John Throckmorton. The Throckmortons of Coughton, with whom he has often been connected, have always been a Roman Catholic family, but he may have been related to the Haseley branch of this family, which was Protestant. This seems the more likely from the fact that Job was a prominent name among the Throckmortons of Haseley and John Throckmorton had a son Job, which name is perpetuated to this day among his descendants. Another conjecture is that he may have descended from the Huntingdonshire branch of the family. John Throckmorton removed to Salem, Mass., and his "hoggehowse" is twice mentioned as a landmark in the town records of 1639. He seems, however, to have left there before that year. While in Salem, if not before, he became a prominent follower of Roger Williams. Under date of July 1st, 1639, "a letter is sent from the church here to the church at Dorchester, notifying them, that they had excommunicated Roger Williams, John Throgmorton, Thomas Olney and Stukely Westcott, with their wives, and Mary Holliman and widow Reeves; because they refused admonition and denied that the churches of the Bay were true churches. It remarks, that all of them but two, had been re-baptized. It states that the following were also cut off: John Elford, William James, John Talby and William Wolcot, the last for neglecting to have his child baptized." (Felt's *Annals of Salem.*) Roger Williams left Salem in 1636, the date of his excommunication, and John Throckmorton must have left in that or the following year and settled in Providence, R. I., for in June, 1637, lands were laid out in the town of Providence and confirmed to several persons "as their proper right and inheritance to them and theirs, as fully as the former portions appropriated to our neighbor Throckmorton, neighbor Greene, neighbor Harris, Joshua Verin, neighbor Arnold and neighbor Williams were, and are confirmed to them or theirs." This seems to show that John Throckmorton was with Roger Williams very near the beginning of the settlement at Providence. On October 8th, 1638, he was one of the twelve persons to whom Roger Williams deeded land that he had bought of the Indian chiefs Canonicus and Miantonomi, and on April 22d, 1639, he bought of Roger Williams his interest in what is now called Prudence Island. He was one of thirty-nine to sign an agreement for a form of government July 27th, 1640. In the autumn of 1642, John Throckmorton left Providence and came with thirty-five families to New Amsterdam with the purpose of settling within the Dutch dominions. Such a petition having been made, Governor Kieft granted the following license October 2d, 1642: "Whereas Mr. Throckmorton, with his associates, solicits to settle with thirty-five families within the limits of the jurisdiction of their High Mightinesses, to reside there in peace and enjoy the same privileges as our other subjects, and be favored with the free exercise of their religion; having seen the petition of the aforesaid Throckmorton, and consulted with the interests of the Company, as this request can by no means be injurious to the country—more so as the English are to settle at a distance of three miles from us—so it is granted. Mr. Throckmorton, with thirty-five English families, are permitted to settle within three miles of Amsterdam." A settlement was made on the East River in what was a part of Westchester County, but now included in the Borough of the Bronx, New York City. It was in the territory which the Dutch had bought of the Indians in 1640 and called Vredeland, meaning "Land of Peace." The settlement now made was called by the Dutch Oostdorp and by the English Easttown. [NOTE.—This is stated on the authority of Scharf in his "History of Westchester County, N. Y.," but the name Oostdorp appears also to have been given to a later settlement perhaps some miles distant from the former, if Scharf has not confused the two.

This is seen in the following extract from a letter sent by the Revs. Johannes Megapolensis and Samuel Drissius to the Classis of Amsterdam, dated August 5th, 1657: "On the west shore of the East River, about one mile beyond Hellgate, as we call it, and opposite Flushing, is another English village, called Oostdorp, which was begun two years ago. The inhabitants of this place are also Puritans or Independents."] A patent was granted for the land on July 6th, 1643. The point known as Throg's Neck, on the end of which Fort Schuyler is now situated, was included within this grant, and its name is undoubtedly an abbreviation of Throgmorton. On October 6th, 1643, the settlement was attacked by the Indians and destroyed, eighteen being killed, and the rest escaping in boats. Some of the Throckmorton children were probably killed in this massacre. The settlement was not rebuilt, but John Throckmorton returned to Providence and in 1652 conveyed the land by permission of the Dutch government to Augustine Hermans. He was a deputy to the provincial legislature from Providence in 1664, 1665, 1666, 1667, 1668, 1670, 1671 and 1673, and was town treasurer in 1677. Though at first an ardent follower of Roger Williams, he became one of the earliest converts of George Fox, the Quaker, during the latter's visit to the colonies. He died in 1687 at Middletown, N. J., while on a visit to his son, and is buried in an unmarked grave in what is now known as the Ancient Lippit or Taylor Burying Ground at Middletown. This is the burying ground mentioned in the will of his son John as follows: "And my will is that one quarter of an acre of land where my father was buried in Middletown shall not be sold, but to remain for a burying place for me and all my posterity and all my relations forever." John Throckmorton had at least seven children, probably more, whose names and children are as follows:

(1) Freegift Throckmorton, died prior to November 8th, 1669.

(2) Patience Throckmorton, born 1640, died September 7th, 1676, married December, 1655, John Coggeshall of Newport, R. I., born 1618, died October 1st, 1708, son of John and Mary Coggeshall. He had been divorced from his first wife, Elizabeth Baulstone (married January 17th, 1647), by act of Assembly on May 25th, 1655, and after his second wife's death he was married a third time to Mary ———. Issue by second wife: Freegift, James, Mary, Joseph, Rebecca, Patience, Benjamin, Content, Content.

(3) John Throckmorton, died July or August, 1690, married December 12th, 1670, Alice Stout, daughter of Richard Stout and Penelope Van Princis. Issue: Joseph, Rebecca, Sarah, Patience, Alice, Deliverance.

(4) Job Throckmorton (a), born September 30th, 1650, died August 20th, 1709, married February 2d, 1685, Sarah Leonard, born at Lynn, Mass., July 30th, 1660 (or June 26th, 1663), died February 5th, 1744, daughter of Henry and Mary Leonard. Issue: John, Rebecca (married Jonathan Holmes), Joseph, Job (b), Mary, Patience, Sarah, Samuel.

(5) Deliverance Throckmorton, married Rev. James Ashton. Issue: James, John, Mary, Alice, Deliverance, Rebecca, Joseph.

(6) Joseph Throckmorton, a mariner, died 1690.

(7) Daughter, married Mr. Taylor.

(b) Job Throckmorton, "Sr.," the son of Job Throckmorton (a) and Sarah Leonard, died February, 1747, married Frances (Stout ?). Issue: John (c), William, Thomas, Mary, Daniel, David, Job, Rebecca, Lewis, Joseph, Elizabeth.

(c) John Throckmorton, of Freehold, probably died 1776, son of Job (b) and Frances Throckmorton, married December 28th, 1739, his cousin, Sarah Holmes, daughter of Jonathan Holmes and Rebecca Throckmorton, born August 18th,

1719, died August 24th, 1805, buried at Holmdel, N. J. Issue:

(1) Sarah Throckmorton, baptized June 30th, 1746, buried November 15th, 1750.

(2) John Throckmorton, baptized October 24th, 1750, when about one year old, buried October 26th, 1750.

(3) James Throckmorton, baptized November 10th, 1751, when two months old.

(4) Rebecca Throckmorton, baptized May 26th, 1754, married Mr. Large.

(5) Sarah Throckmorton, born December 11th, 1757, died unmarried March 8th, 1805.

(6) Holmes Throckmorton (d), baptized April 22d, 1759, buried October 4th, 1821, married Susannah Forman, died 1820.

(d) Holmes Throckmorton lived at Tinton Falls, where he was the owner not only of a large farm but also of a number of slaves. During the Revolutionary War he was a private in Spencer's Regiment in the Continental Army. Issue:

(1) John Throckmorton, marrried Mary Serviss. Issue: Joseph, Isaac, Susan, Mary, Forman, Charles.

(2) Sarah Throckmorton, married John Obart. Issue: George, Throckmorton, Nancy, Susan, Jane.

(3) Forman Throckmorton, married April 9th, 1812, Elizabeth Morris. Issue: Sarah Forman, William, Charles Forman, Ann Matilda, Jane, Susan, Charlotte, John Wilson, James Forman.

(4) Jane Throckmorton, born April 13th, 1791, died August 18th, 1885, married April 1st, 1810, William Scott [621*]. Issue: Catherine, Susan, John, Sarah Ann, Holmes Throckmorton, Jane Amanda, Mary Caroline, William Webster.

(5) Joseph Throckmorton, died unmarried.

(6) Holmes Throckmorton, died unmarried.

(7) Elizabeth Throckmorton, married John Britton. Issue: John, Mary, Catherine. She married a second time and went West.

(8) Mary Throckmorton, born October 31st, 1808, died 1899, married John Wilson, died August 8th, 1859. Issue: Forman, George, Catherine, Holmes Throckmorton, Charles Henry, William Forman, Susan, Sarah, Mary Jane, James K., John, Mary Ann, Frank.

THE HOLMES FAMILY.

Rev. Obadiah Holmes, born 1607 at Preston, Lancashire, England, died 1682, married Catherine ———. He came to this country about 1639, in which year he lived at Salem, Mass., and was engaged in the manufacture of glass with Lawrence Southwick and Annanias Conklin. He joined the Baptists, and on account of his connection with them was indicted in 1650. On July 31st, 1651, Obadiah Holmes and John Clarke were arrested for conducting a Baptist meeting at William Witter's house, Lynn, Mass., and were sentenced by the court to pay a fine of £30, or to be publicly whipped. Obadiah Holmes refused to pay his fine on the ground that it would be a confession of error, and after being kept in prison until September, "he was severely whipped in public in Boston with a three corded whip thirty lashes." He later settled near Newport, R. I., where he became pastor of the Baptist church. He was one of the Monmouth patentees, but never resided in New Jersey. Some of his children settled in this colony, however, and many of his descendants are among its present inhabitants. His children were as follows:

(1) Mary Holmes, married John Brown.

(2) Martha Holmes, born 1640.

(3) Samuel Holmes, born 1642, died 1679, married 1665 Alice Stillwell, born 1645; resided at Gravesend, L. I. Issue: Samuel, Joseph, Anne, Katharine, Mary.

(4) Obadiah, born 1644, married ———

Cole; resided successively at Middletown, N. J., Staten Island, N. Y., and Cohansey, N. J. Issue: Obadiah, Samuel, Jonathan and two daughters.

(5) Lydia Holmes, married Captain John Bowne. Issue: John, Obadiah, Deborah, Sarah, Catherine.

(6) Jonathan Holmes (a), married Sarah Borden.

(7) John Holmes, born 1649, died 1712, married 1st, 1671, Frances Holden, born 1649, died 1679; married 2d, 1680, Mary Greene, born 1652, died 1713, widow of William Greene.

(8) Hopestill Holmes, married ——— Taylor.

(a) Jonathan Holmes, died 1713, married Sarah Borden, born 1644, died 1705; resided at Middletown, N. J. Issue: Obadiah (b), Jonathan (c), Samuel, Sarah, Mary, Catherine, Martha, Lydia, Joseph.

(b) Obadiah Holmes, died April 3d, 1745, married 1696 Alice Ashton, born 1671, died 1716, daughter of James Ashton and Deliverance Throckmorton. He was sheriff of Monmouth County in 1699. Issue: Jonathan (d), Obadiah, James, Samuel, Joseph, John, Deliverance wife of Joseph Smith, and Mary wife of James Mott.

(d) Jonathan Holmes, died 1770, married Teuntje Hendrickson, daughter of Daniel Hendrickson. Issue:

(1) Obadiah Holmes, baptized October 28th, 1716, died unmarried 1752.

(2) Daniel Holmes, baptized April 9th, 1721, married 1752 Leah Bowne, born 1736, died March 15th, 1813, daughter of James Bowne and Margaret Newbold.

(3) Jonathan Holmes, baptized July 19th, 1722, married 1758 Sarah Potter.

(4) Joseph Holmes, died 1763, married June, 1752, his cousin, Sarah Mott, daughter of James Mott and Mary Holmes.

(5) John Holmes, married 1764 Catherine Brown.

(6) Alice Holmes, baptized March 30th, 1730, died May 19th, 1796, married 1749 John VanBrackle.

(7) Catherine Holmes, born May 11th, 1731, died May 12th, 1796, married 1st, 1749, Hendrick Schenck, born July 29th, 1731, died August 24th, 1766, son of Roelof Schenck and Geesye Hendrickson; married 2d John Schenck, died February 13th, 1775, son of Garret Schenck and his third wife Neeltje Voorhees. Issue (all by first marriage): Roelof, born April 17th, 1752, died October 12th, 1800, married Sarah Schenck; Sarah, born May 26th, 1755, died June 30th, 1758; Mary, born March 17th, 1757, married Jacob Covenhoven; Jonathan, born July 19th, 1761, died April 4th, 1771; Catherine, born March 17th, 1762, died unmarried June 5th, 1816; Eleanor, born March 17th, 1764, married George Crawford [62]; Ann, born June 14th, 1766, married Jonathan Holmes, son of Samuel Holmes.

(8) Mary Holmes.

(9) James Holmes, baptized Jacobus May 1st, 1737.

(10) Samuel Holmes, baptized July 8th, 1739.

(11) William Holmes, died 1776.

(c) Jonathan Holmes, born 1681, died December 26th, 1766, married 1st Deliverance Ashton, daughter of James Ashton and Deliverance Throckmorton; married 2d Rebecca Throckmorton, born 1691, died November 10th, 1761, daughter of Job Throckmorton and Sarah Leonard. Issue (all but the first two by second wife):

(1) Jonathan Holmes, died unmarried 1738.

(2) Deliverance Holmes, married Peter Bowne.

(3) Sarah Holmes, born August 18th, 1719, died August 24th, 1805, married December 28th, 1739, her cousin, John Throckmorton, died 1776, son of Job and Frances Throckmorton. Issue: Sarah, John, James, Rebecca wife of ——— Large, Sarah, Holmes.

(4) Joseph Holmes, born December 15th, 1721, died March 23d, 1738.

(5) Samuel Holmes, born October 4th, 1726, died November 29th, 1769, married 1745 Mary Stout, born 1727, died April

23d, 1773. Issue: Samuel, John S., Jonathan, Joseph, Elisha, Stout, Lydia wife of Garret Stillwell, Parmelia wife of —— Stillwell, and Catherine wife 1st of —— Hegeman and 2d of Nathan Stout.

(6) Obadiah Holmes.

(7) John Holmes, born July 27th, 1730, died unmarried August 26th, 1804.

(8) Rebecca Holmes, born March 4th, 1734, died June 24th, 1757, married March 2d, 1756, Gilbert, or Gibeon, Tice. Issue: Rebecca wife of ——— Bachelder.

THE VAN BRUNT FAMILY.

Rutger Joesten Van Brunt (son of Joost or George Van Brunt), the first ancestor of the Van Brunt family in America, came from Holland in 1653 and was among the first settlers in New Utrecht, L. I., in 1657. In 1661 he was a member of the Court of Schepens, and in 1678-80 was one of the principal magistrates under the English government. He married for his first wife Tryntje Claes, widow of Stoffel Harmensen Van Borculo, and died intestate prior to 1713. Issue by this marriage: Nicholas, Joost or George, and Cornelius (a).

(a) Cornelius Rutgersz Von Brunt was a farmer and lived in New Utrecht. He was an elder in tbe Dutch Church of New Utrecht from 1715 to 1731, a member of the Colonial Legislature of New York from 1698 to 1731, and a justice of the peace in Kings County from 1712 to 1718. He married December 18th, 1685, Tryntje, a daughter of Adrain Williamsen Bennett of Gowanus. His will, dated July 25th, 1748, was proved May 13th, 1754. He had a son, Nicholas Van Brunt (b).

(b) Nicholas VanBrunt, the progenitor of the VanBrunts of Monmouth County, N. J., married Geesye Hendrickson, a sister of Daniel Hendrickson, who was the first settler of this name at what is now Holland in Holmdel township. The old records of the Marlboro Dutch Church show that Nicholas VanBrunt and his wife became communicants there in 1731, and thus probably settled in Monmouth County about that time. In 1750 he bought of Robert Hunter Morris a tract of 600 acres at Tinton Falls. His will, dated April 12th, 1760, was proved February 1st, 1782, and is recorded at Trenton. He had nine children as follows: Hendrick, Cornelius (c), Nicholas, Catherine, Jannetje, Anne, Engeltje (baptized April 27th, 1732), Augenetje (baptized March 9th, 1734) wife of Albert Schenck, and Geesye (baptized October 23d, 1737).

(c) Cornelius VanBrunt married about 1750 Magdalena Fenton. Issue: Hendrick (baptized May 7th, 1752), Cornelius (baptized January 28th, 1754), Nicholas, Joseph C. (d), and Geesye wife of Okey Hoagland.

(d) Joseph C. VanBrunt, youngest son of Cornelius VanBrunt, married Mary Applegate and resided in Shrewsbury. His daughter Ann VanBrunt (called *Polly* in Bergen's VanBrunt Family) married 1st March 12th, 1813, James Scott [622], and 2d February 1st, 1829, William I. Matthews, and died prior to 1868.

VI.

John White and Mary Scott.

16. MARY[2] SCOTT, born August 30th, 1712, married 1st, marriage license dated September 13th, 1729, Thomas Tollet of Burlington, and married 2d, marriage license dated June 25th, 1739, JOHN WHITE of Shrewsbury, died prior to 1796. (See Monmouth County Deeds, O, 7.) Issue:

1401. JOB[3] WHITE.

1402. HANNAH[3] WHITE, married Garret Covenhoven; resided in Bethlehem township, Hunterdon County, N. J.

1403. SARAH[3] WHITE, married ——— Gasper, died prior to 1796; resided in Somerset County, N. J.

1404. CATHERINE[3] WHITE, married, license dated April 28th, 1778, Samuel Scott [2202*], died 1822, probably son of Ebenezer Scott and Patience Leonard; resided in Montgomery township, Somerset County, N. J.

1405. AARON[3] WHITE, died 1801, married, license dated October 2d, 1780, Deborah Trafford. He was a carpenter by trade, and resided at different times in New York City and at Shrewsbury, N. J.

VII.

Samuel Scott and Amy Borden.

17. SAMUEL[2] SCOTT, born August 11th, 1715, died July, 1785, married 1st April 14th, 1736, Almy, or Amy, Borden, born February 6th, 1715, daughter of Francis and Mary Borden of Shrewsbury; married 2d, license dated September 13th, 1758, Sarah Allen of Shrewsbury, who survived him. Francis Borden, the father of his first wife, was the son of Francis Borden and Jane Vickers, and grandson of Richard Borden and Joan Fowler. Samuel Scott lived on one of the Scott plantations inherited from his father near Newman's Spring, part of which is now included in the borough of Red Bank. His will, dated July 5th, 1785, was proved July 25th, 1785 (Trenton Wills, 27, 145). He had seven children, all by his first wife, six of whom were living at the time of his death. Issue:

1501*. ELIZABETH[3] SCOTT, married Edmund Lafetra.

1502*. HANNAH[3] SCOTT, born 1742, married William Pintard.

1503*. EBENEZER[3] SCOTT, born November 7th, 1744, married Elizabeth ——.

1504. JOHN[3] SCOTT, died unmarried 1817, called "Laughing John" on account of his constant good humor; resided in Shrewsbury township. His will, dated April 16th, 1787, was presented to the Monmouth County Orphans' Court in 1817, at the October term, because of the informality that it had no witnesses. The will was allowed, and both of the executors named therein being dead, administration was granted to Samuel Pintard [1541] October 21st, 1817. In this will John Scott divides his estate into three shares, one of which he leaves to his brother Ebenezer, one to his sister Hannah, and the other to be equally divided among the children of his sister Elizabeth. The division of the real estate was made and reported to the Court at the January term, 1822.

1505. JANE[3] SCOTT, died unmarried 1786.

1506. AMY[3] SCOTT, died unmarried 1822.

1507. WILLIAM[3] SCOTT, married Ann ——, and with his wife and brother John Scott [1504] signed a deed in 1800. This marriage may be the one recorded where William Scott married January 31st, 1799, Nancy Allen, but that is by no means certain.

1501. ELIZABETH[3] SCOTT, married December 11th, 1766, Edmund Lafetra, born November 6th, 17-9, son of James Lafetra and Hannah Brower. Edmund Lafetra married 2d Sarah Potter, and by her had four children. He lived at Shrewsbury. The children by his first wife were as follows:

1511. EDMUND[4] LAFETRA, a twin, born September 27th, 1767, died October 24th, 1838, unmarried.

1512. HANNAH[4] LAFETRA, a twin, born September 27th, 1767, married John[4] Pintard [1546*].

1513. AMY[4] LAFETRA, born March 12th, 1769, died March 29th, 1834, unmarried.

1514*. ELIZABETH LAFETRA, born January 29th, 1771, married Daniel Allen.

1514. ELIZABETH[4] LAFETRA, born January 29th, 1771, married Daniel

The Quaker Meeting House at Shrewsbury.

Allen, possibly the son of Joseph and Hannah Allen. Issue:

1521. JOHN[5] ALLEN.

1522. ELIZABETH[5] ALLEN, married William Smith.

1523. SARAH[5] ALLEN, married ——— Leon.

1524*. EBENEZER[5] ALLEN, born March 1st, 1801, married Ann Little.

1525. CATHERINE[5] ALLEN, married Nathaniel Myers.

1524. EBENEZER[5] ALLEN, born March 1st, 1801, died April 3d, 1877, married March 4th, 1828, Ann Little. Issue:

1531. ELIZABETH[6] ALLEN, born March 9th, 1829, married Daniel Cook.

1532. CATHERINE[6] ALLEN, baptized November 9th, 1834, married Jacob H. Morris.

1533. HANNAH[6] ALLEN, baptized April 9th, 1837, married George Allard.

1534. SARAH[6] ALLEN, married 1st Ernest Butell and 2d Abram Brown.

1535. MARY LOUISA[6] ALLEN, born February 20th, 1839, married George Githens.

1536. THOMAS H. B.[6] ALLEN, born June 11th, 1841, married Hannah Sherman.

1537. JEROME[6] ALLEN, married Antoinette Shafto.

1538. CHARLES[6] ALLEN, married Prudence Rebecca Reynolds.

1502. HANNAH[3] SCOTT, born 1742, died February 18th, 1792, married, license dated January 5th, 1761, William Pintard of Shrewsbury, born 1733, died March 3d, 1809, son of Samuel and Ann Pintard, and grandson of Anthony Pintard, a Huguenot, who came to Shrewsbury from the West Indies in 1687, whither he is supposed to have fled from France after the revocation of the Edict of Nantes. Issue:

1541. SAMUEL[4] PINTARD, born September 14th, 1762, died October 7th, 1833, married Deborah Wall, born October 30th, 1766, died October 12th, 1847.

1542. AMY[4] PINTARD, baptized December 1st, 1765, and was living in 1832, married ——— Millet.

1543*. GLENCROSS[4] PINTARD, born 1767, married Catherine Slocum.

1544. ANN[4] PINTARD, born 1772, died August 5th, 1819, unmarried.

1545*. WILLIAM[4] PINTARD, born May, 1776, married Lydia Holmes.

1546*. JOHN[4] PINTARD, born 1779, married Hannah[4] Lafetra [1512].

1547*. HANNAH[4] PINTARD, born August 19th, 1783, married Samuel Tilton.

1543. GLENCROSS[4] PINTARD, born 1767, died April 28th, 1835, married Catherine Slocum, born March 1st, 1782, died March 30th, 1869, daughter of Samuel Slocum and his second cousin Susanna Slocum. The will of Glencross Pintard, dated March 20th, 1835, was proved May 12th, 1835 (Monmouth County Wills, C, 475). Issue:

1551. ELIZA[5] PINTARD, born February 14th, 1804, died unmarried.

1552. SUSAN[5] PINTARD, born May 11th 1805, died unmarried.

1553*. CATHERINE[5] PINTARD, born September 6th, 1806, married Pierce Hill.

1554. JOHN[5] PINTARD, born March 20th, 1808, married in Onondaga county, N. Y.

1555. ANN[5] PINTARD, born August 20th, 1809, married Joshua Bailey.

1556. SAMUEL[5] PINTARD, born May 18th, 1811.

1557. CAROLINE[5] PINTARD, born January 22d, 1813 (?), died November 5th, 1873, married 1st, March 1st, 1842, William[5] Pintard [1601], and 2d ——— Whitlock.

1558*. EUGENE[5] PINTARD, born October 26th, 1815, married 1st Elizabeth Parker, and 2d Deborah E. Chadwick.

1559. SARAH[5] PINTARD, born November 23d, 1818, died unmarried.

1560. AMELIA M.[5] PINTARD, born July 29th, 1824, died unmarried July, 1882.

1553. CATHERINE[5] PINTARD, born September 6th, 1806, died January 15th, 1888, married Pierce Hill. Issue:

1561. ELIZA PINTARD[6] HILL.

1558. EUGENE[5] PINTARD, born October 26th, 1815, died December 20th, 1880, married 1st, September 7th, 1843, Elizabeth Parker, born November 15th, 1804, died August 21st, 1854, daughter of William Parker and Elizabeth Woolley; married 2d Deborah E. Chadwick, born 1824, died April 17th, 1903, daughter of Tabor Chadwick; resided at Little Silver, N. J. He had the four following children, all but the last by his first wife:

1571. EUGENE[6] PINTARD, living unmarried at Little Silver, N. J.

1572. WILLIAM[6] PINTARD, living unmarried in Philadelphia.

1573. CAROLINE[6] PINTARD, living unmarried at Little Silver, N. J.

1574*. IDA[6] PINTARD, married Orlando Worden.

1574. IDA[6] PINTARD, married Orlando Worden. Issue:

1581. ORLANDO[7] WORDEN.

1582. HOWARD[7] WORDEN, born 1887.

1583. CHARLES[7] WORDEN.

1584. EUGENE[7] WORDEN.

1585. ETHEL[7] WORDEN, born 1896.

1545. WILLIAM[4] PINTARD, born May, 1776, died January 27th, 1852, married Lydia Holmes. Issue:

1591. SAMUEL HOLMES[5] PINTARD, born November 26th, 1811.

1592. ANN[5] PINTARD, born May 30th, 1813, died March 10th, 1872, married Herbert Coleman, born November 15th, 1808, died November 11th, 1868.

1546. JOHN[4] PINTARD, born 1779, died August 19th, 1856, married his cousin HANNAH[4] LAFETRA [1512], born September 27th, 1767, died December 21st, 1842, daughter of Edmund Lafetra and Elizabeth[3] Scott [1501]. Issue:

1601. WILLIAM[5] PINTARD, born July, 1801, died November 8th, 1850, married 1st Elizabeth———, and 2d March 1st, 1842, Caroline[5] Pintard [1557].

1602. MARSDEN[5] PINTARD, baptized August 26th, 1821, as adult; married December 16th, 1827, Mary Allen.

1603. HANNAH[5] PINTARD, born September 5th, 1805, died February 3d, 1863, unmarried.

1604*. DEBORAH[5] PINTARD, born May 24th, 1807, married Samuel Dorn.

1604. DEBORAH[5] PINTARD, born May 24th, 1807, died May 4th, 1862, married Samuel Dorn, born July 21st, 1805, died September 4th, 1866. Issue:

1611. THEODORE[6] DORN, baptized October 2d, 1842.

1612. WILLIAM PINTARD[6] DORN, born May 18th, 1843.

1613. JOHN MARSDEN[6] DORN, born November 18th, 1845.

1614. HANNAH CAROLINE[6] DORN, born October 7th (or 5th), 1846, died August 15th, 1873.

1615. SAMUEL[6] DORN, born April 29th, 1850, died February 4th, 1851.

1547. HANNAH[4] PINTARD, born August 19th, 1783, died April 20th, 1842, married Samuel Tilton, born January 6th, 1777, died May 17th, 1861, son of Clayton and Catherine Tilton. Samuel Tilton married 2d Susan Squires, born 1796, died October 28th, 1864, widow of Captain Squires of St. John, N. B. Issue by first marriage:

1621. JOHN[5] TILTON, born April 12th, 1802, died March 18th, 1820.

1622. MARY ANN[5] TILTON, died unmarried at the age of 86 years.

1623. MERCY[5] TILTON, married Thomas Alphonso McGlade.

1624. CATHERINE[5] TILTON, born 1811, died unmarried December 20th, 1869.

1625. DEBORAH[5] TILTON, married James F. Earle.

1626*. HANNAH PINTARD[5] TILTON, born March 21st, or 22d, 1816, married Sheppard Kollock.

1627. CHARLOTTE AMELIA[5] TILTON,

born June 1st, 1821, married Charles Wetmore[5] Scott [1668*].

1628*. ELIZABETH CORNELIA[5] TILTON, married Sheppard Kollock.

1626. HANNAH PINTARD[5] TILTON, born March 21st, or 22d, 1816, died March 20th, 1853, married November 9th, 1833, Sheppard Kollock, born August 19th, 1813, son of Isaac Arnett Kollock and Elizabeth Cox, who is still living (1907) at Red Bank, N. J. Issue:

1631. ELIZABETH MARY[6] KOLLOCK, born January 31st, 1836, married Thomas K. Durham.

1632. JOHN ANTHONY[6] KOLLOCK, born December 25th, 1837, died January 8th, 1839.

1633. JOHN PINTARD[6] KOLLOCK, born July 5th, 1840, died June 22d, 1846.

1634. HANNAH TILTON[6] KOLLOCK, baptized August 28th, 1842, married Charles K. Bishop, and died one year after marriage; no issue.

1635. AMELIA GERTRUDE[6] KOLLOCK, born July 7th, 1844, married John B. Hurd.

1636. JOHN HENRY[6] KOLLOCK, baptized December 20th, 1846, married 1st Emma Whitney, married 2d Mrs. Dorn (nee Force), a widow, and married 3d, ——— Cottrell.

1637. EDWIN WALTER[6] KOLLOCK, baptized July 22d, 1849, married Florence Shakleford. He is a minister of the Protestant Episcopal Church and resides at Sewaren, N. J.

1638. FLORENCE FINCH[6] KOLLOCK, baptized November 25th, 1852, died young.

1639. EMELINE[6] KOLLOCK, married Charles K. Bishop, the husband of her deceased sister Hannah [1634], as his second wife.

1628. ELIZABETH CORNELIA[5] TILTON, married 1854 Sheppard Kollock, the husband of her deceased sister Hannah [1626], as his second wife. Issue:

1641. CHARLOTTE C.[6] KOLLOCK, married John M. Meredith.

1642. CATHERINE TILTON[6] KOLLOCK, unmarried.

1643. SHEPPARD[6] KOLLOCK, married Emma McGinty.

1644. ANNIE LAURENCE[6] KOLLOCK, died young.

1645. ANNIE ARNETT[6] KOLLOCK.

1503. EBENEZER[3] SCOTT, born November 7th, 1744, died May, 1817, married Elizabeth ———, born March 8th, 1742, died June 9th, 1815; removed to St. John, New Brunswick, Canada, in 1783, where he died. His will, dated April 30th, 1817, was filed at Freehold March 20th, 1818 (Monmouth County Wills, G, 402). Issue:

1651*. SAMUEL[4] SCOTT, born September 18th, 1771, married Elizabeth Tilton.

1652*. ANN[4] SCOTT, married John Mount.

1651. SAMUEL[4] SCOTT, born September 18th, 1771, went with his father to St. John, New Brunswick, in 1783, and died there intestate April 28th, 1817; married Elizabeth Tilton, born July 15th, 1783, died 1816, daughter of Clayton and Catherine Tilton. Issue:

1661. ANN ELIZABETH[5] SCOTT, born May 3d, 1804.

1662. JOHN[5] SCOTT, born March 9th, 1806, resided in New Brunswick, Canada, where he probably has descendants.

1663. JOSEPH[5] SCOTT, born February 24th, 1808, died prior to April 30th, 1817, as he is not mentioned in his grandfather's will of that date.

1664*. WILLIAM[5] SCOTT, born April 4th, 1810.

1665. EBENEZER[5] SCOTT, born March 30th, 1812, married Charlotte ———; resided in New York City, where he was living in 1843; no issue.

1666. CLAYTON[5] SCOTT, a twin, born June 18th, 1814.

1667. CATHERINE[5] SCOTT, a twin, born June 18th, 1814.

1668*. CHARLES WETMORE[5] SCOTT, born January 29th, 1816, married 1st

Charlotte Amelia Tilton, and 2d Mary Emeline Covert.

1664. WILLIAM[5] SCOTT, born April 4th, 1810, married and resided in New Brunswick, Canada. Issue:
1671. ALICE[6] SCOTT.
1672. WILLIAM[6] SCOTT.

1668. CHARLES WETMORE[5] SCOTT, born January 29th, 1816, at St. John, N. B., married 1st, January 5th, 1843, his second cousin, Charlotte Amelia[5] Tilton [1627], born June 1st, 1821, died October 1st, 1845, daughter of Samuel Tilton and Hannah[4] Pintard [1547]; married 2d Mary Emeline Covert, born October 18th, 1830, died April 2d, 1874. He resided in Shrewsbury township, near Red Bank. There was one child by the first marriage, ten by the second, as follows:
1681. THOMAS ALPHONSO[6] MCGLADE, JR., born September 16th, 1844, died unmarried July 27th, 1884, so-called because adopted by Thomas Alphonso McGlade, the husband of his mother's sister Mercy [1623]. He was a lawyer by profession.
1682*. ELIZABETH BARKER[6] SCOTT, born July 19th, 1847, married James Clayton.
1683*. CHARLES HARMER[6] SCOTT, born April 23d, 1849, married Frances A. Wood.
1684. LOUISA[6] SCOTT, born 1851, married Thomas J. Marcellus; no issue.
1685*. BLOOMFIELD[6] SCOTT, born February 9th, 1854, married Augusta Markwalter.
1686*. MARY EMMA[6] SCOTT, born April 20th, 1857, married George B. Decker.
1687*. LAURA L.[6] SCOTT, born June 9th, 1859, married Abram B. Salter.
1688*. EBENEZER[6] SCOTT, born October 19th, 1860, married Elizabeth B. Denise.
1689*. WILLIAM[6] SCOTT, born August 4th, 1863, married Mamie Le Maistre.
1690. GEORGE W.[6] SCOTT, born March 10th, 1867, (or March 9th, 1866), died January 4th, 1878.
1691. CATHERINE B.[6] SCOTT, born February 25th, 1870, died in infancy.

1682. ELIZABETH BARKER[6] SCOTT, born July 19th, 1847, married March 9th, 1873, James Clayton, born December 16th, 1834, died February 13th, 1882, son of Japhia Clayton and Margaret Thompson; resides at Red Bank, N. J. Issue:
1701. ALICE M.[7] CLAYTON, born March 29th, 1874, died January 11th, 1878.
1702. JAMES MARCELLUS[7] CLAYTON, born November 5th, 1878.
1703*. HARRY HANCOCK[7] CLAYTON, born December 18th, 1880, married Elena Coley.

1703. HARRY HANCOCK[7] CLAYTON, born December 18th, 1880, married April 16th, 1902, Elena Coley, daughter of Captain George Coley and Mary Girard. Issue:
1711. GEORGE[8] CLAYTON, born March 27th, 1906.

1683. CHARLES HARMER[6] SCOTT, born April 23d, 1849, died 1888, married December 18th, 1876, Frances A. Wood, born March 12th, 1860. He was engaged in newspaper work, and was the founder of the *Amenia Times* at Amenia, N. Y. His family reside at Red Bank, N. J. Issue:
1721. FLORENCE[7] SCOTT, born August 16th, 1879, married July 26th, 1906, Seymour Day.
1722. LOUISE MARCELLUS[7] SCOTT, born June 5th, 1882.
1723. CLAYTON WETMORE[7] SCOTT, born September 22d, 1884.
1724. AUGUSTA FOUNTAIN[7] SCOTT, born August 21st, 1886.

1685. BLOOMFIELD[6] SCOTT, born February 9th, 1854, died June 8th, 1904, at Los Angeles, Cal., married Augusta Markwalter of Atlanta, Ga., daughter of Michael Markwalter and Elizabeth Clay. Issue:
1731*. EULA MAY[7] SCOTT, born Decem-

ber 11th, 1879, married Dr. Charles A. Meade.

1732. CHARLES M. W.[7] SCOTT, born March 25th, 1881, married July 18th, 1905, Daisy May White, born June 10th, 1883, daughter of John White; reside at Long Branch, N. J.

1733*. LILLIAN[7] SCOTT, born February 1st, 1883, married Phineas Ulhrich.

1734. LIONEL[7] SCOTT, born February 5th, 1892.

1731. EULA MAY[7] SCOTT, born December 11th, 1879, died July 22d, 1906, married 1905 Dr. Charles A. Meade, a surgeon by profession. Issue:

1741. GRACE LILLIAN[8] MEADE, born January 16th, 1906.

1733. LILLIAN[7] SCOTT, born February 1st, 1883, married February 13th, 1905, Phineas Ulhrich; reside at Los Angeles, Cal. Issue:

1751. EULA LEAH[8] ULHRICH, born October 15th, 1906.

1686. MARY EMMA[6] SCOTT, born April 20th, 1857, married November 7th, 1877, George B. Decker, born September 25th, 1855, son of Abram Decker and Sarah Smith; resides at Red Bank, N. J. Issue:

1761*. MABEL F.[7] DECKER, born September 1st, 1878, married William Johnston.

1762. GEORGE B.[7] DECKER, born September 9th, 1880.

1763*. ABRAM[7] DECKER, born September 24th, 1882, married Grace Hill.

1764. DOROTHY[7] DECKER, born June 4th, 1885.

1765. CLARENCE L.[7] DECKER, born April 26th, 1897, died March 15th, 1898.

1761. MABEL F.[7] DECKER, born September 1st, 1878, married William Johnston. Issue:

1771. HARRY[8] JOHNSTON.

1763. ABRAM[7] DECKER, born September 24th, 1882, married Grace Hill. Issue:

1781. MONROE[8] DECKER.

1687. LAURA L.[6] SCOTT, born June 9th, 1859, married October 15th, 1884, Abram B. Salter, born March 2d, 1856, son of Anthony P. and Clarissa Salter; reside at Bayonne, N. J. Issue:

1791. ANTHONY[7] SALTER, born August 22d, 1885, deceased.

1792. BESSIE C.[7] SALTER, born August 3d, 1887.

1793. GRACE A.[7] SALTER, born May 9th, 1889.

1688. EBENEZER[6] SCOTT, born October 19th, 1860, married March 5th, 1884, Elizabeth B. Denise, born January 15th, 1867, daughter of Samuel T. Denise and Elizabeth Dangler; reside at Red Bank, N. J. Issue:

1801. LESTER WALLACK[7] SCOTT, born December 25th, 1884.

1802. EVA CLAFLIN[7] SCOTT, born October 18th, 1893.

1689. WILLIAM[6] SCOTT, born August 4th, 1863, married Mamie Le Maistre; reside at Red Bank, N. J. Issue:

1811. ELLEN[7] SCOTT.

1652. ANN[4] SCOTT, married John Mount; she went with her father in 1783 to St. John, New Brunswick, Canada, where she died before 1819. Issue:

1821. MARY[5] MOUNT.

1822. SUSAN[5] MOUNT.

1823. ELIZA[5] MOUNT.

VIII.

John Scott and Ruth Stockton.

19. JOHN[2] SCOTT, born November 3d, 1719, married, license dated September 29th, 1746, Ruth Stockton, daughter of Richard Stockton, who was a farmer in Somerset County. This Richard Stockton was the son of Richard and Susanna Stockton, and grandson of Richard and Abigail Stockton. John Scott was a mason by trade. Receiving money, not land, as his share of his father's estate, he settled in Windsor township, Middlesex County. He was living in 1766, and is known to have had at least two sons as given below, and possibly a daughter Mehitable. Issue:

1901. SAMUEL[3] SCOTT, about whom little is known except that he was still living in 1824, and, like his father, was a mason by trade.

1902*. RICHARD[3] SCOTT, married Lydia ———.

1903. MEHITABLE[3] SCOTT, married, license dated August 27th, 1779, John Melrose of Somerset County, N. J.

1902. RICHARD[3] SCOTT, died 1786, married Lydia ———; resided at Princeton, N. J. His will, dated April 17, 1786, was proved November 8th, 1786. (Trenton Wills, 29, 191.) Issue:

1911. SUSANNAH[4] SCOTT. She may have been the one who married August 12th, 1800, Joseph Norman.

1912*. JOB[4] SCOTT, born 1775, married.

1913. MEHITABLE[4] SCOTT.

1912. JOB[4] SCOTT, born 1775, married ———. Issue:

1921*. ANNA[5] SCOTT, married 1st ——— Fetters, 2d ——— Hull, and 3d ——— Allen.

1922*. SARAH[5] SCOTT, married (William?) Scott.

1923*. RACHEL[5] SCOTT, married John Burrows.

1924*. BENJAMIN[5] SCOTT, married 1st Beulah———, 2d Sarah A. Knows, and 3d Mary S. Grover.

1921. ANNA[5] SCOTT, married 1st ——— Fetters, 2d———— Hull, and 3d———— Allen of Philadelphia. Issue:

1931. RACHEL[6] FETTERS.

1932. THOMAS[6] ALLEN.

1922. SARAH[5] SCOTT, married (William?) Scott; resided in Philadelphia. Issue:

1941. CHARLES[6] SCOTT.

1923. RACHEL[5] SCOTT, married John Burrows; resided in Philadelphia. Issue:

1951. MARY JANE[6] BURROWS; resides at Palmyra, N. J.

1952. MATILDA[6] BURROWS; resides at Palmyra, N. J.

1953. RACHEL[6] BURROWS, deceased, married ———— Booth.

1954. WILLIAM[6] BURROWS, died unmarried.

1955. A son, died young.

1924. BENJAMIN[5] SCOTT, married 1st Beulah ————, died about six months after marriage; married 2d Sarah A. Knows, born September 25th, 1807, died July 16th, 1843; married 3d Mary S. Grover, born October 1st, 1818,

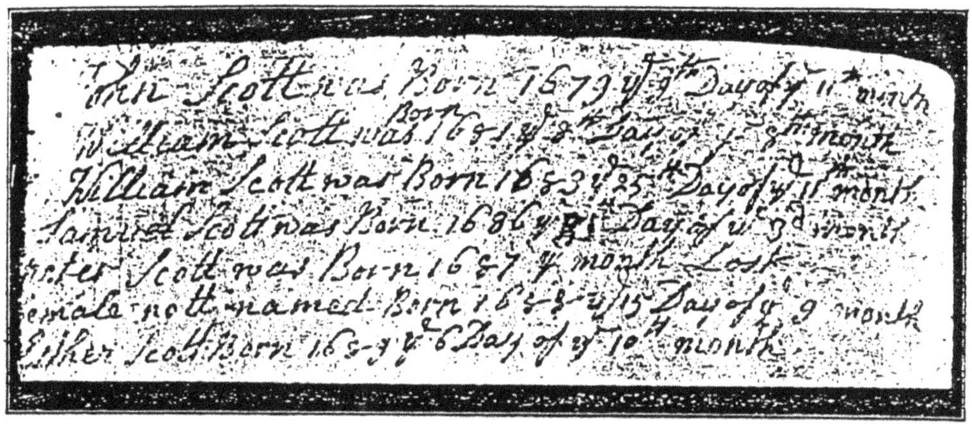
John Scott was Born 1679 ye 9th Day of ye 11th month
William Scott was Born 1681 ye 8th Day of ye 8th month
William Scott was Born 1683 ye 25th Day of ye 11th month
Samuel Scott was Born 1686 ye [illegible] Day of ye 3d month
Peter Scott was Born 1687 4 month Lost
female not named Born 1688 ye 15 Day of ye 9 month
Esther Scott Born 1689 ye 6 Day of ye 10th month

THE OLDEST BIRTH RECORDS FOUND WRITTEN IN BARCLAY'S "APOLOGY FOR QUAKERS," BEING THE CHILDREN OF WILLIAM SCOTT AND ABIGAIL TILTON WARNER. WHERE THESE DIFFER FROM THE SHREWSBURY QUAKER RECORDS, THE LATTER HAVE BEEN FOLLOWED (SEE PAGE 13.)

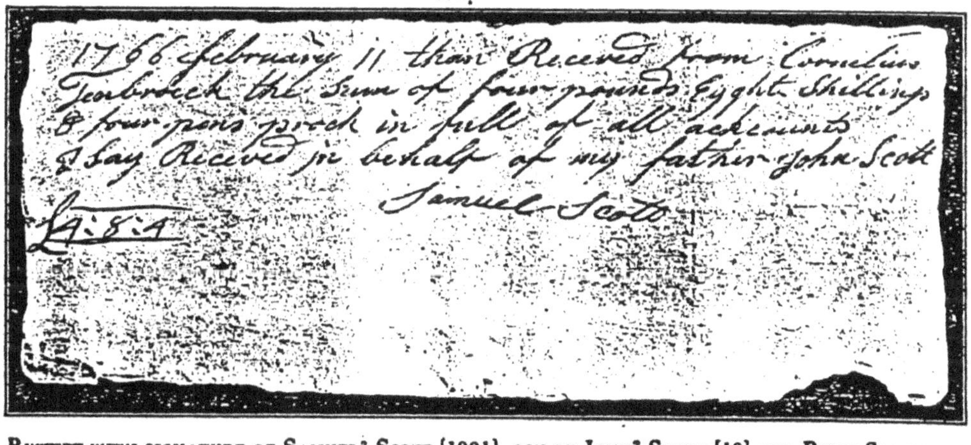
1766 february 11 than Received from Cornelius Tenbroeck the Sum of four pounds Eyght Shillings & four pens proch in full of all accounts I say Received in behalf of my father John Scott
Samuel Scott
£4:8:4

RECEIPT WITH SIGNATURE OF SAMUEL[3] SCOTT [1901], SON OF JOHN[2] SCOTT [19] AND RUTH STOCKTON.

died April 21st, 1878; resided at Plainsboro, N. J. He had thirteen children, six by his second, and seven by his third marriage, as follows:

1961*. ANNA A.[6] SCOTT, born 1826, married William H. Tindall.

1962*. JACOB K.[6] SCOTT, born 1831, married Mary G. Dey.

1963*. BENJAMIN A.[6] SCOTT, married Susan Embley.

1964*. JOB ASHLEY[6] SCOTT, married 1st ——— Griggs, and 2d ——— VanArsdale.

1965*. EMILY[6] SCOTT, married John Hullfish.

1966. THOMAS[6] SCOTT, married Josephine Keeler; resides in Trenton and has one son.

1967*. REBECCA[6] SCOTT, born December 7th, 1844, married Nathaniel Britton.

1968. RICHARD[6] SCOTT, married Susan Mount; reside in Illinois; no issue.

1969. MARY[6] SCOTT, resides in Trenton, N. J.

1970*. KENNETH D.[6] SCOTT, married Anna James.

1971. JOHN[6] SCOTT, unmarried.

1972*. WILLIAM T. A.[6] SCOTT, born April 25th, 1857, married Emma Hammell.

1973. HOWARD[6] SCOTT, unmarried.

1961. ANNA A.[6] SCOTT, born 1826, died 1895, married William H. Tindall, born 1818, died 1860. Issue:

1981. BENJAMIN[7] TINDALL.

1982. SARAH[7] TINDALL, married Hugh L. Reabey, Esq.; reside at Mt. Vernon, N. Y.

1983. EMILY[7] TINDALL.

1984. JOHN P.[7] TINDALL, born 1857, died 1865.

1962. JACOB K.[6] SCOTT, born 1831, married Mary G. Dey, born 1834, died 1897, resides at Trenton, N. J. Issue:

1991. ELLA[7] SCOTT, died August 8th, 1857, aged 5 months 8 days.

1992*. EMMA[7] SCOTT, married Jacob Perrine.

1993*. FRED[7] SCOTT, married Susanna Updyke.

1994*. ELLA[7] SCOTT, married William Wiley.

1995*. LAURA[7] SCOTT, born March 12th, 1867, married Elmer Grover.

1996*. HARRY N.[7] SCOTT, married Lottie Perrine.

1992. EMMA[7] SCOTT, married Jacob Perrine. Issue:

2001. GEORGE[8] PERRINE.

1993. FRED[7] SCOTT, married Susanna Updyke. Issue:

2011. STELLA[8] SCOTT.

2012. WALTER[8] SCOTT.

2013. FLORA[8] SCOTT.

2014. ALVA[8] SCOTT.

1994. ELLA[7] SCOTT, married William Wiley. Issue:

2021. FRANKLIN[8] WILEY.

1995. LAURA[7] SCOTT, born March 12th, 1867, married April 25th, 1888, Elmer Grover, born May 25th, 1865; reside near Plainsboro, N. J. Issue:

2031. ALFRED LEE[8] GROVER, born April 19th, 1889.

2032. BEULAH E.[8] GROVER, born December 9th, 1890.

2033. ELMER RUSSELL[8] GROVER, born January 19th, 1894.

1996. HARRY N.[7] SCOTT, married Lottie Perrine; reside near Cranbury, N. J. Issue:

2041. ERNEST[8] SCOTT.

2042. HAROLD[8] SCOTT.

1963. BENJAMIN A.[6] SCOTT, died 1898, married Susan Embley; resided at Plainsboro, N. J. Issue:

2051. WALTER[7] SCOTT, married ——— Schenck; resides at Plainsboro, N. J.

2052. FRANK[7] SCOTT, married ——— Russell.

2053. ALBERT B.[7] SCOTT, married.

2054. RACHEL[7] SCOTT, deceased.

1964. JOB ASHLEY[6] SCOTT, married

1st ——— Griggs, and married 2d ——— VanArsdale; resided in Somerville, N. J. Issue by first marriage:

2061. MARGARET[7] SCOTT, married George Hoagland.

1965. EMILY[6] SCOTT, married John Hullfish. Issue:

2071. HOWARD[7] HULLFISH.

2072*. CATHERINE[7] HULLFISH, married 1st ——— Russell, and 2d Dr. Lindsay.

2072. CATHERINE[7] HULLFISH, married 1st ——— Russell, and 2d Dr. Lindsay of Ohio. Issue:

2081. VALERIA[8] RUSSELL.

1967. REBECCA[6] SCOTT, born December 7th, 1844, married March 5th, 1863, Nathaniel Britton, born February 19th, 1841, son of Col. Dean Britton and Mary Scott Dey; reside near Plainsboro, N. J. Issue:

2101. MARIETTA[7] BRITTON, born January 2d, 1864, married Charles W. Riggs; resides in Trenton, N. J.

2102. ELIZABETH C.[7] BRITTON, born November 28th, 1865, married Charles Okeson; reside near Kingston, N. J.

2103. LAURA W.[7] BRITTON, born September 18th, 1867, married Frank Johnson; reside in Princeton, N. J.

2104. CATHERINE L.[7] BRITTON, born December 6th, 1869, married Enoch Mount; reside at Morrisville, N. J.

2105. NATHANIEL[7] BRITTON, born March 4th, 1872, died June 28th, 1895.

2106. JOHN D.[7] BRITTON, born October 2d, 1874, married Nellie Rue, sister of Charles Rue.

2107. LOUISA B.[7] BRITTON, born December 12th, 1878, married Emerson Bodine; reside near Dayton, N. J.

2108. MAUD E.[7] BRITTON, born September 6th, 1880, married Charles Rue; reside at Plainsboro, N. J.

2109. WAHNIETA[7] BRITTON, born October 27th, 1883, married Frank Macmamee; reside at Plainsboro, N. J.

1970. KENNETH D.[6] SCOTT, married Anna James; reside at Princeton, N. J. Issue:

2111. CHARLES[7] SCOTT, married Matilda———, and is a druggist in Trenton, N. J.

2112. BENJAMIN HERBERT[7] SCOTT.

2113. FREDERICK[7] SCOTT.

1972. WILLIAM T. A.[6] SCOTT, born April 25th, 1857, died July 15th, 1889, married Emma Hammell. Issue:

2121. WILLIAM[7] SCOTT, born December 25th, 1886, died January 4th, 1887.

IX.

Ebenezer Scott and Patience Leonard.

21. EBENEZER[2] SCOTT, born May 17th, 1723. died 1760, married, license dated October 1st, 1748, Patience Leonard. He appears to have settled near his brother John in Windsor township, Middlesex County. (See Trenton Wills, G, 320.) He had at least one son James and a daughter Rachel, and probably the two other children mentioned below, though not in that order. Issue:

2201*. JAMES[3] SCOTT, born February 9th, 1751, married Margaret VanCleaf.

2202*. RACHEL[3] SCOTT, born April 19th, 1760, married Lewis Conover.

2203*. SAMUEL[3] SCOTT, married Catherine White [1404].

2204*. WILLIAM[3] SCOTT, married.

2201. JAMES[3] SCOTT, born February 9th, 1751, died January 12th, 1816, married May 16th, 1774, Margaret VanCleaf, born February 1st, 1753, died July 16th, 1839, daughter of Benjamin and Leanah VanCleaf. He resided at Freehold, N. J., "on the road leading from Middletown Point to the Monmouth Court House." His will, dated June 30th, 1812, was proved March 11th, 1816. (Monmouth County Wills, A, 736.) Issue:

2211. WILLIAM[4] SCOTT, born September 25th, 1774, died unmarried November 14th, 1841; resided on his father's homestead farm at Freehold.

2212. LENAH[4] SCOTT, born September 16th, 1776, died November 16th, 1793.

2213. HANNAH[4] SCOTT, born June 4th, 1779, died January 13th, 1859, married February 27th, 1804, James VanKirk, and was living a widow in Warren County, Ohio, in 1847.

2214*. PATIENCE[4] SCOTT, born July 6th, 1781, married 1st Peter H. Conover and 2d Garrett Wyckoff.

2215. SARAH[4] SCOTT, born May 16th, 1783, died unmarried February 23d, 1861; resided at Freehold and in Marlboro township, Monmouth County. Her will, dated February 22d, 1859, was proved March 25th, 1861. (Monmouth County Wills, G, 361.)

2216*. EBENEZER[4] SCOTT, born April 29th, 1785, married 1st Eliza Thompson and 2d Ann Knott Little.

2217. BENJAMIN[4] SCOTT, born April 20th, 1788, died unmarried March 30th, 1861; resided at Freehold, N. J.

2218*. DEBORAH[4] SCOTT, born December 24th, 1792, married William Little.

2219. JAMES[4] SCOTT, born February 17th, 1795, died unmarried April 4th, 1872; resided at Freehold and Matawan, N. J.

2214. PATIENCE[4] SCOTT, born July 6th, 1781, died April 24th, 1845 (or 1847), married 1st June 12th, 1816, Peter H. Conover, born April 18th, 1778, died August 14th, 1817, being his second wife; married 2d January 8th, 1834, Garrett Wyckoff, as his second wife. Garrett Wyckoff, born May 14th, 1758, died May 10th, 1850, was the son of Garrett Wyckoff and Patience Williamson, and was a soldier in the Revolutionary War, being made a prisoner when only seventeen years of age and confined in a prison ship in New York harbor. Issue by first marriage:

2231*. MARY P.[5] CONOVER, born May 27th, 1817, married Aaron Vanderveer.

2231. MARY P.[5] CONOVER, born May 27th, 1817, died February 12th, 1886, married October 30th, 1838, Aaron Vanderveer, born March 7th, 1815, died January 16th, 1887, son of Joseph I. Vanderveer and Jane Smock. Issue:

2241. JOSEPH AUGUSTUS[6] VANDERVEER, born January 11th, 1840, married January 8th, 1863, Rachel M. Rue.

2242*. PETER CONOVER[6] VANDERVEER, born July 31st, 1844, married A. Eliza Herbert.

2243. ANN[6] VANDERVEER, born June 29th, 1847, died August 4th, 1896, married December 13th, 1866, David Abeel Statesir.

2244. SARAH SCOTT[6] VANDERVEER, born April 13th, 1854, died May 29th, 1884, married August 26th, 1874, Rev. Abram J. Beekman.

2242. PETER CONOVER[6] VANDERVEER, born July 31st, 1844, died April 4th, 1900, married December 26th, 1867, A. Eliza Herbert, born July 4th, 1848, died April 1st, 1901. Issue:

2251*. WILLIAM HERBERT[7] VANDERVEER, born February 24th, 1870, married Ida May Conover [2748].

2252. CHARLES C.[7] VANDERVEER, born September 4th, 1873, died unmarried August 9th, 1898.

2251. WILLIAM HERBERT[7] VANDERVEER, born February 24th, 1870, married May 26th, 1897, Ida May Conover [2748], born May 28th, 1866, daughter of John B. Conover and Mary Ann Smock; reside at Freehold, N. J. Issue:

2261. MARYAN CONOVER[8] VANDERVEER, born January 4th, 1901.

2262. WILLIAM HERBERT[8] VANDERVEER, born August 18th, 1902, died February 11th, 1904.

2263. CHARLES HERBERT[8] VANDERVEER, born August 17th, 1905.

2216. EBENEZER[4] SCOTT, born April 29th, 1785, died March 26th, 1858, married 1st August 5th, 1824, Eliza Thompson, and married 2d September 18th, 1836, Ann Knott Little of Howell, probably died 1844, daughter of Joseph Knott and widow of William Little, whom she had married April 30th, 1814. Ebenezer Scott resided for a time at Middletown, and after his second marriage at Howell. He appears to have had at least the following children:

2271. MARGARET[5] SCOTT, who was living in 1844.

2272*. WALTER[5] SCOTT, married.

2272. WALTER[5] SCOTT, who married and went West, residing at St. Louis, Mo., and in California. Issue:

2281. WILLIAM[6] SCOTT, who resides at St. Louis, Mo.

2218. DEBORAH[4] SCOTT, born December 24th, 1792, died August 26th, 1876, married January 9th, 1814, William Little, born January, 1780, in County Cavan, Ireland, died January 8th, 1864. He was first cashier, then president, of the Farmers and Merchants' Bank of Middletown Point, now Matawan, where he resided, and the first school here was started by him. Issue:

2311. JAMES[5] LITTLE, born November 30th, 1814, died unmarried March 1st, 1843.

2312. WILLIAM S.[5] LITTLE, born January, 1822, died August 8th, 1822.

2313. HENRY STAFFORD[5] LITTLE, born August 17th, 1823, died unmarried April 24th, 1904. He was graduated from Princeton University in 1844, and was admitted to the bar in 1848. He was state senator from Monmouth County nearly three terms from 1864 to 1872, when he resigned his seat to become clerk of the Court of Chancery.

2314*. MARGARET SCOTT[5] LITTLE, born September 25th, 1825, married William L. Terhune.

2315. SARAH FRANCES[5] LITTLE, born June 6th, 1831, died August 15th, 1838.

2314. MARGARET SCOTT[5] LITTLE, born September 25th, 1825, died December 30th, 1906, married October 10th, 1843, William L. Terhune, born May 16th, 1815, died December 27th, 1907. He was a lawyer by profession, being admitted to the bar in 1838, and resided at Matawan, N. J. Issue:

2321*. JAMES LITTLE[6] TERHUNE, married 1st Mary Anna White and 2d Helen Louise White.

2322. WILLIAM LITTLE[6] TERHUNE, born 1849, died January 5th, 1869.

2323. MARY GREENLEAF[6] TERHUNE, born 1853, died November 28th, 1856.

2324*. JOHN[6] TERHUNE, married Fanny Brown.

2325. HENRY STAFFORD[6] TERHUNE, married Mary W. Crane. He resides at Matawan, but is engaged in the practice of law at Long Branch, N. J. He has been state senator from Monmouth County.

2326. MARGARET LITTLE[6] TERHUNE, resides at Matawan.

2321. JAMES LITTLE[6] TERHUNE, married 1st Mary Anna White, daughter of Gordon Dennis White and Catherine Jane Smock; married 2d Helen Louise White, a sister of his first wife. He resides at Matawan, and is president of the First National Bank of Red Bank, N. J. Issue by first marriage:

2331. HELEN LOUISE[7] TERHUNE.

2324. JOHN[6] TERHUNE, married Fanny Brown. He resides at Matawan, and is cashier of the First National Bank of Long Branch, N. J. Issue:

2341. KATHRYN B.[7] TERHUNE.

2202. RACHEL[3] SCOTT, born April 19th, 1760, died April 5th, 1813, married April 9th, 1781, Lewis Conover, born September 1st, 1752, died May 27th, 1843, son of Peter Conover and Anna Davis, and a descendant of Wolfert Garretse Van Couwenhoven, who came to this country from Amersfoost, Utrecht, Holland, in 1630. They resided at Rumson and Freehold, N. J. Rachel Scott was born in the year her father died, and was brought up by her aunt, Hannah[2] Scott [18], the wife of John Williams, who mentions her in his will. She is not therefore the one who married George Gardner, as suggested on page 15. Lewis Conover was a soldier in the Revolutionary War, and carried orders for General Washington at the Battle of Monmouth. Issue:

2351. JOSEPH[4] CONOVER, born January 17th, 1782.

2352*. EBENEZER[4] CONOVER, born October 15th, 1783, married Mary Lefferson.

2353. HANNAH[4] CONOVER, born September 18th, 1785.

2354. MARY[4] CONOVER, born May 8th, 1788.

2355. PATIENCE[4] CONOVER, a twin, born September 10th, 1790, died May, 1791.

2356. DEBORAH[4] CONOVER, a twin, born September 10th, 1790.

2357. ANNE[4] CONOVER, born March 26th, 1800.

2358. HELENA[4] CONOVER, born April 11th, ——.

2352. EBENEZER[4] CONOVER, born October 15th, 1783, died November 18th, 1857, married December 17th, 1807, Mary Lefferson, born November 19th, 1784, died March 16th, 1861, daughter of Ockey Lefferson and Sarah Schenck; resided near Freehold, N. J. His will, dated January 15th, 1853, was proved November 30th, 1857. (Monmouth County Wills, G, 77.) Issue:

2361*. SARAH[5] CONOVER, born November 7th, 1808, married Nathan H. Jackson.

2362*. RACHEL[5] CONOVER, born December 4th, 1810, married Adam Conrow.

2363*. JANE[5] CONOVER, born April 7th, 1813, married Levi S. Sutphin.

2364*. WILLIAM E.[5] CONOVER, born October 14th, 1815, married Charlotte Baker.

2365*. JAMES SCOTT[5] CONOVER, born October 2d, 1818, married Frances E. Meeker.

2366*. MARY ANN[5] CONOVER, born September 14th, 1821, married Aaron Sutphin.

2367*. ARTHUR L.[5] CONOVER, born April 18th, 1824, married Catherine Thompson.

2368*. JOHN B.[5] CONOVER, born November 22d, 1829, married Mary Ann Smock.

2361. SARAH[5] CONOVER, born November 7th, 1808, died February 28th, 1884, married May 15th, 1828, Nathan H. Jackson, born August 15th, 1805, died February 3d, 1854. Issue:

2371. WILLIAM H.[6] JACKSON, born February 21st, 1829, married 1st February 22d, 1853, Mary V. Applegate, born September 1st, 1832, died February 24th, 1873; married 2d April 21st, 1875, Sarah A. Job Perrine, born October 31st, 1833. Issue, all but the last by first marriage: William Franklin, Edwin Augustus, Sarah Louisa, Marianna, Laura, Jennie, Ada.

2372. EDWARD[6] JACKSON, born December 1st, 1830, died May 24th, 1835.

2373. MARY ANN[6] JACKSON, born November 16th, 1832, died September 5th, 1896.

2374. EBENEZER C.[6] JACKSON, born November 19th, 1835, died February 16th, 1904, married September 13th, 1859, Mary Frances Sillcocks, born July 31st, 1837. Issue: William Eben, Rebecca M., Charles Warren, Frederick H., George Conover, Anna L., Howard B.

2375. REBECCA[6] JACKSON, born October 13th, 1838, died April 15th, 1864, married September 18th, 1861, Walter O. Woodford, born February 27th, 1836, died April 13th, 1882. Issue: Walter Emerson (married Matilda J. Perrine).

2376. NATHAN MORRIS[6] JACKSON, born September 7th, 1844, died June 2d, 1861.

2377. EDWIN AUGUSTUS[6] JACKSON, born November 22d, 1851, died June, 1854.

2362. RACHEL[5] CONOVER, born December 4th, 1810, died April, 1901, married February 25th, 1835, Adam Conrow, born July 11th, 1810, died May 6th, 1859. Issue:

2411. JAMES W.[6] CONROW, born February 28th, 1836, died August 26th, 1903, married October 15th, 1860, Mary E. Moore, born April 5th, 1838. Issue: Florence Louise, Robert White, Mabel Thompson.

2412. MARY[6] CONROW, born June 6th, 1838, married July 11th, 1867, James Hanford, born May 31st, 1824, died December 7th, 1901.

2413. WILLIAM E.[6] CONROW, born September 17th, 1840, died May 16th, 1902, married April 16th, 1868, Anna M. Hanford, born March 7th, 1847. Issue: Dora Louise, Anna Hanford, Wilford Seymour.

2414. THEODORE[6] CONROW, born December 14th, 1844, married April 15th, 1873, Helen J. Stillwell, born September 20th, 1852. Issue: Effie Clarke, Helen Clare.

2415. SARAH FRANCES[6] CONROW, born February 14th, 1848, married October 4th, 1866, John H. Francis, born August 20th, 1843. Issue: Minnie, Bertram.

2416. LOUISA[6] CONROW, born February 6th, 1851, married October 27th, 1874, Theodore D. Anderson, born June 24th, 1849. Issue: Lillian Conrow, Catherine Voorhies.

2363. JANE[5] CONOVER, born April 7th, 1813, died November 15th, 1842, married February 24th, 1836, Levi S. Sutphin, born October 27th, 1813, died September 3d, 1866. Issue:

2471. WILLIAM E.[6] SUTPHIN, born September 19th, 1837, married September 24th, 1868, Louise Ely Conover, born October 6th, 1841. Issue: Fannie Bunting, Kate Louise, William Craig.

2472. JOSEPH HALSEY[6] SUTPHIN, born August 17th, 1840, married October 16th, 1879, Susan Cooley Hulbert, born June 28th, 1857. Issue: Josephine Hulbert, Henry Hulbert, Dorothy.

2473. CATHERINE LOUISE[6] SUTPHIN, born October 29th, 1842, died March 19th, 1905, married November 17th, 1864, William A. Hankinson, born March 14th, 1840. Issue: Jennie Augusta, Fred Stolley.

2364. WILLIAM E.[5] CONOVER, born October 14th, 1815, died August 24th, 1891, married February 5th, 1839, Charlotte Baker, born January 27th, 1817, died September 29th, 1874, daughter of Jacob Baker of Englishtown, N. J.; resided near Freehold, N. J. Issue:

2511. CHARLES H. W.[6] CONOVER, born July 31st, 1840, married November 23d, 1865, Cordelia Vaughn, born March 5th, 1841; reside at Flint, Michigan. Issue: Charlotte, Estella, Mary Frances, Charles Vaughn.

2512. EBENEZER[6] CONOVER, born January 30th, 1842, died August 29th, 1868, married February 21st, 1867, Evelina Hartshorne, born December 14th, 1844. Issue: Warren Hartshorne (married Annie Barkalow Conover).

2513. JACOB BAKER[6] CONOVER, born May 8th, 1844, died January 20th, 1906, married December 24th, 1868, Mary Virginia Reid, born October 3d, 1846. Issue: William Reid, Charles E., Nellie Frances, Charlotte May, Elizabeth V., Mary Jane.

2514. MARY JANE[6] CONOVER, born March 10th, 1846.

2515. WILLIAM PERRINE[6] CONOVER, born October 3d, 1848, died October 5th, 1850.

2516. ANNA L.[6] CONOVER, born September 2d, 1850.

2517. ELIZABETH V.[6] CONOVER, born July 18th, 1852, married September 26th, 1877, John Leguir Many, born May 6th, 1852; reside at New Orleans, La. Issue: Ralph Conover (Cecil Rhodes scholar at Oxford University, died March 23d, 1908), John Leguir, Anna Estelle.

2518. FRANCES[6] CONOVER, born August 1st, 1854, married October 22d, 1884, William Segoine, born July 16th, 1839; reside at Point Pleasant, N. J. Issue: Frances Elizabeth, Harold Richard, Marion.

2519. JAMES MADISON[6] CONOVER, born February 11th, 1857.

2520. LEWIS[6] CONOVER, born February 10th, 1858, died March 16th, 1858.

2521. NATHAN JACKSON[6] CONOVER, born April 8th, 1860.

2522. CHARLOTTE[6] CONOVER, born August 11th, 1861, died July 2d, 1867.

2365. JAMES SCOTT[5] CONOVER, born October 2d, 1818, died September 3d, 1894, married April 17th, 1843, Frances E. Meeker, born December 4th, 1825, died September 15th, 1897. Issue:

2581. ALONZO EDWARD[6] CONOVER, born June 7th, 1844, married June 7th, 1866, Lena Rebecca Underhill, born January 16th, 1847. Issue: Alonzo Edward, Florence Lena, Clarence Underhill, Lillian Frances.

2582. JAMES WILSON[6] CONOVER, born January 29th, 1846, died August 23d, 1847.

2583. WILLIAM EDGAR[6] CONOVER, born November 3d, 1847, died February 13th, 1902, married December 10th, 1873, Sarah Louise Holley, born August 9th, 1849. Issue: Edgar Everest, William Seymour, James Scott, Frances Elizabeth, Lawrence Seymour, Marjorie Elsie.

2584. FRANKLIN[6] CONOVER, a twin, born August 5th, 1849, died August 15th, 1850.

2585. EUGENE[6] CONOVER, a twin, born August 5th, 1849, died August 4th, 1850.

2586. CLARENCE SCOTT[6] CONOVER, born September 11th, 1852, died April 29th, 1856.

2587. EDWIN MEEKER[6] CONOVER, born December 17th, 1854, died May 30th, 1856.

2588. FRANCES ELIZABETH[6] CONOVER, born December 21st, 1856, died March 24th, 1870.

2589. MARY EMMA[6] CONOVER, born October 9th, 1863, died February 2d, 1865.

2366. MARY ANN[5] CONOVER, born September 14th, 1821, died March 15th, 1900, married Aaron Sutphin, born July 16th, 1813, died October 10th, 1870. Issue:

2611. WILLIAM H.[6] SUTPHIN, born August 29th, 1842, married February 25th, 1869, Emma Sharpe, born September 12th, 1847. Issue: DeWitt B., William C.

2612. ELIZABETH[6] SUTPHIN, born June 9th, 1844, died December 2d, 1878, married February 27th, 1868, Wykoff G. Conover, born January 28th, 1844. Issue: Mary Louise, Anna H., Sarah, Eva S.

2613. MARY JANE[6] SUTPHIN, born September 29th, 1846, died April 24th, 1904.

2614. AARON R.[6] SUTPHIN, born September 6th, 1849, married June 1st, 1881, Lelia E. Condray, born August 12th, 1862. Issue: Edwin A., Charles C., Helen Ray.

2615. JOHN F.[6] SUTPHIN, born March 27th, 1852, died April 29th, 1856.

2616. EDWIN J.[6] SUTPHIN, born June 21st, 1854, married May 26th, 1892, May Josephine Hamilton, born June 8th, 1868. Issue: Edwin J., Elsie E., Clarence Hamilton, Earle Franklin.

2617. CHARLES[6] SUTPHIN, born January 18th, 1857, married 1st December 4th, 1881, Justina Pittinger, born April 26th, 1860, died January 31st, 1888; married 2d October 22d, 1889, Mary F. Butler, born March 8th, 1858. Issue, two by the first, and five by the second marriage: Edwin J., Emma J., Charles J., Francis A., Walter Lewis, Mary Jane, John Almer.

2618. JAMES G.[6] SUTPHIN, born February 11th, 1859, married May 15th, 1883, Lizzie M. Walker, born January 7th, 1860. Issue: Lulu May, James A.

2367. ARTHUR L.[5] CONOVER, born April 18th, 1824, died August 14th, 1899, married December 15th, 1847, Catherine Thompson, born June 21st, 1825, died March 26th, 1908. Issue:

2681. JOHN R.[6] CONOVER, born March 17th, 1850, married April 26th, 1882, Emily M. Robinson, born June 14th, 1843. Issue: F. Ethel, Hewlett R., Emma D. M.

2682. MARY C.[6] CONOVER, born October 2d, 1852, married December 25th, 1872, William W. Antonides, born April 31st, 1844. Issue: Carrie, John R., Laura, Fannie W., Myrtle, Florence, William, Leroy C., Arthur, Howard V., Charles L., Henry C.

2683. SARAH F.[6] CONOVER, born July 31st, 1855, married October 29th, 1874, A. M. T. Flandreau, born April 28th, 1839. Issue: Kate C., Arthur C., Daniel A., Harold H., Wilbur A., Grace M.

2684. JOANNA[6] CONOVER, born September 10th, 1857, married March 16th, 1883, Frank C. Fenton, born July 14th, 1857. Issue: Frank A.

2685. HENRY A.[6] CONOVER, born January 6th, 1861, married October 1st, 1884, Helen M. Gardiner, born March 23d, 1861. Issue: James Scott, Gardiner.

2686. WILLIAM[6] CONOVER, born August 10th, 1865, died August 31st, 1865.

2368. JOHN B.[5] CONOVER, born November 22d, 1829, married December 9th, 1852, Mary Ann Smock, born December 9th, 1829, died November 24th, 1907; resides near Freehold, N. J. Issue:

2741. JANE ANN[6] CONOVER, born October 20th, 1853.

2742. MARY AUGUSTUS[6] CONOVER, born December 7th, 1855, died August 27th, 1870.

2743. SARAH ELIZABETH[6] CONOVER, born December 14th, 1857, married October 2d, 1879, Charles Dubois Forman, born November 3d, 1853. Issue: Margaretta, Helen C.

2744. ELLA S.[6] CONOVER, a twin, born July 18th, 1860, married February 9th, 1882, Henry Conover Wikoff, born October 4th, 1859. Issue: Edgar Emmons, Frederick Conover.

2745. EMMA H.[6] CONOVER, a twin, born July 18th, 1860, married May 19th,

PATIENCE[4] SCOTT [2216], WHO MARRIED 1ST PETER H. CONOVER AND 2ND GARRETT WYCKOFF. FROM A MEDALLION IN THE POSSESSION OF MR. W. HERBERT VANDERVEER, ONE OF HER DESCENDANTS.

1881, Charles Parker Emmons, born April 9th, 1858.

2746. GEORGE B.[6] CONOVER, born December 16th, 1862, married March 22d, 1893, Isabella F. Roahr, born June 1st, 1864.

2747. KATE LOUISE[6] CONOVER, born February 5th, 1865, died February 23d, 1865.

2748. IDA MAY[6] CONOVER, born May 28th, 1866, married William Herbert Vanderveer [2281*].

2749. HENRIETTA[6] CONOVER, born October 4th, 1868, died October 11th, 1896.

2750. FRANK J.[6] CONOVER, a twin, born April 29th, 1872, married October 10th, 1903, Grace Huxford.

2751. FLORENCE[6] CONOVER, a twin, born April 29th, 1872, died August 3d, 1872.

2203. SAMUEL[3] SCOTT, died 1822, married, license dated April 28th, 1778, Catherine White [1404], daughter of John White and Mary Scott [16]; resided in Montgomery township, Somerset County, N. J. His will, dated January 30th, 1817, was proved April 16th, 1822. (Somerset County Wills, C, 86.) Issue:

2781. AARON[4] SCOTT. It is possible that Samuel Scott [2203] had a son by this name, who was living in 1794, but who probably died prior to 1817. (See Middlesex County Deeds, 16, 461.)

2782. JESSE[4] SCOTT, died unmarried, 1833. His will, dated November 29th, 1832, was proved June 18th, 1833. (Somerset County Wills, D, 320.)

2204. WILLIAM[3] SCOTT, married ——. Issue:

2791. SAMUEL[4] SCOTT.

2792. JOHN[4] SCOTT.

APPENDIX.

Here are placed a few records, not mentioned elsewhere in this work, which concern persons who may have a place in the family, the certainty of which, however, has not been definitely ascertained.

WILLS.

Will of John Scott of Somerset Co. April 5th, 1808. Moses Scott, son of Benjamin Scott, my nephew. Job Scott, second son of the above named Benjamin Scott, both of Bucks Co., Pa. John Scott Price, now a minor, son of Mary Stiff, my granddaughter. Daughter Susannah Stiff. Proved June 21st, 1808.—Somerset Co. Wills, A, 174.

Will of Martin Scott of Six Mile Run, Franklin township, Somerset Co. October 24th, 1819. I "bequeath unto my mother, Amy Scott, all that lot of woodland lying in the County of Middlesex I drawed as an heir of my father, William Scott, as divided by the Commissioners appointed by Law to make a dividend of the Estate of my aforesaid father, William Scott." Undivided right in his father's New York lands bequeathed to brothers and sisters. Brothers Samuel and John. Sisters Eliza and Mary Ann. Proved November 30th, 1819.—Somerset Co. Wills, B, 326. See Minutes of Middlesex Co. Orphans' Court, B, 109.

Will of Nancy Scott of the City of New Brunswick. 1847. Niece Eliza S. Garretson and her two youngest brothers. Niece Jane G. Gulick. Niece Nancy S. Gulick. Half sister Catherine Gulick. Proved February 21st, 1848.—Middlesex Co. Wills, E, 55.

GUARDIANSHIPS.

October 20th, 1819. Samuel Pintard appointed guardian of Herbert Scott of Monmouth County, minor.—Monmouth Co. Guardianship Records, A, 423.

June 16th, 1862. William H. Conover, Jr., appointed guardian of Alphonso Scott of New York City, a minor over fourteen years of age.—Minutes of Monmouth Co. Orphans' Court, Q, 164.

MARRIAGES.

MONMOUTH COUNTY.

John Roberts and Hannah Scott, March 4th, 1811.

Benjamin Scott of Middletown and Maria Sanford of Shrewsbury, August 18th, 1824.

Henry Roberts and Elizabeth, daughter of Benjamin Scott of Middletown, January 30th, 1842.

George H. Vannabrick of Fillmore and Martha Ann Scott of Allentown, September 25th, 1869.

MIDDLESEX COUNTY.

William Scott and Martha Brown of township of East Windsor, November 10th, 1808.

Peter T. Smith and Mary Scott, October 15th, 1818.

SOMERSET COUNTY.

Samuel W. Scott and Ann Vorhees, September 19th, 1816.

Jacob Scott and Elizabeth Cox, October 5th, 1828.

George W. Scott and Minerva S. Paiste, November 16th, 1839.

A family by the name of Scott has resided in Middletown township, but it is not known that this family is connected with the Scott family of Shrewsbury. A John Scott was living in Middletown township in 1828 and prior, and in that year his son John H. Scott, with Sarah his wife, went to Trumansburg, N. Y. A letter describing this trip by way of the Erie Canal is in the possession of the compiler. (See also Monmouth Co. Deeds, Q, 160.)

INDEX OF PERSONS.

Many names occur more than once on a page.

INDEX.

www.ingramcontent.com/pod-product-compliance
Lightning Source LLC
Chambersburg PA
CBHW081200270326
41930CB00014B/3229